COW - PROTECTION IN INDIA

COW - PROTECTION IN INDIA

L. L. SUNDARA RAM

GYAN

Published by

Gyan Publishing House
5, Ansari Road
Daryaganj, New Delhi-110002
Phone: 011-47034999, 9811692060
E-mail: books@gyanbooks.com

Distribution Network
gyanbooks.com
India, USA, Canada, UK, Australia

ISBN: 978-93-6433-150-0 (PB)

First Published, 1927

2nd Impression 2024

Printed at: Gyan Press, Delhi.

COW - PROTECTION IN INDIA
Author: L. L. SUNDARA RAM

COW-PROTECTION IN INDIA

COW - PROTECTION
IN INDIA

BY

L. L. SUNDARA RAM, M. A.,

Fellow of the Royal Economic Society (London.)

THE SOUTH INDIAN HUMANITARIAN LEAGUE,

George Town, MADRAS.

1927.

CONTENTS

CONTENTS

DEDICATED

WITH KIND PERMISSION

TO

THE ANDHRA UNIVERSITY

AND

HER FIRST VICE-CHANCELLOR

MR. C. RAMALINGA REDDI.

PREFACE

The purpose of this monograph is primarily educative and secondarily constructive. My aim in undertaking this task is to brush away popular misunderstandings regarding the many side-issues of the problem of Cow-protection in India, and present them in their proper perspective.

No one can gainsay the fact that the problem of Cow-protection is quite vague and vast to confuse the activities of even the most enthusiastic of cow-protectors in India. In the first place, there is the religious issue about the place of the cow in the various theories of cosmology forwarded by the different religions of the world. Allied with it is the question of the theological sanction of cow-slaughter for sacrificial purposes. The next issue is that of the sentimental clinging of the masses to traditions and dogmas,—the rigidity of social relationships between the communities embracing different religions in India. Thirdly, there is the humanitarian instinct in man to sanctify life, human as well as animal, which emphasises all the more the importance of conserving cow-life. Lastly, there is the economic nexus of the problem of Cow-protection to the higher interests of the nation. With these main divisions in view, I endeavoured to collect material, sift them and form conclusions,—all the while supporting my views by weighty authorities to show that I am not flying after sentimental platitudes, but only expressing considered opinions formed after a reasoned investigation.

In this volume the first three aspects of the problem are treated in their proper historic perspective. Throughout the whole course of my investigations, my primary aim was to ascertain truth, truth in all its nakedness. My orthodox friends may disagree with me first when I collate evidence in the chapter on the Hindu Attitude to show that at one time in India cow slaughter for sacrificial purposes, besides being tolerated, was deemed essential, and secondly in the chapter on the History of Cow Protection in India where I tried to show that Muhammadan sovereigns of medieval India, including Aurangzib, who is alleged to be the worst enemy of the Hindu religion, attempted to protect cow-life. But truth must be told. But I take shelter under the argument that with the recognition of the above sets of facts the problem of Cow-protection would be solved, in as much as our Muhammadan neighbours would pause first a little before taking to cow slaughter and try to arrive at a correct estimate of the factors that induced our Aryan forefathers to do away with cow slaughter with a view to subserve national interests, and finally to place it under a religious ban, and, secondly, to emulate themselves at the example set by the more liberal of their co-religionists in medieval India. I hope to fulfil shortly the more ambitious task of writing a companion volume on the economic aspects of Cow-protection.

No one is more conscious of the defects of this volume than myself. Being the first systematic attempt after the exposition of the problem of Cow-protection in India many topics of interest and importance might have escaped my notice, while other points might not have been given the benefit of more detailed information. I invite all generous criticism to help me to understand the problem aright in all its phases.

I acknowledge with thanks my obligations to Professor S. Radhakrishnan, M. A., King George V. Professor of Philosophy in the Calcutta University, who has done me the honour of perusing the manuscript and gave me the benefit of his erudition and experience. Dr. V. Shiva Ram, M. A., Ph. D., Head of the Department of Political Science, Lucknow University, has heard the text of the monograph in part and enriched me with his criticism. Dr. I. J. S. Taraporewala, B. A., Ph.D., Professor of Comparative Philology, Calcutta University, has kindly read with appreciative interest the chapter on the teachings of Zarathustra, and helped me to correct a few of my notions about the same. Mr. Muhammad Marmaduke Picthall, Editor of *Islamic Culture*, the Hyderabad Quarterly, and the well-known author of several works on Islam, helped me with a note on the Muslim attitude towards Cow-protection, arriving at substantially identical conclusions, with my own, which has been appended to my chapter on the Muslim Outlook. Professor M. Venkatarangaiya, M. A., Chief Professor of History and Economics, Maharajah's College, Vizianagaram helped me with the manuscript in several ways. To Srijut K. Ramakoteswara Rao, Vice-Principal of the National College, Masulipatam, I owe not only facilities for study and research, but also the final draft of the manuscript. I must also thank my cousin Mr. J. Venkatachala Sarma, B. A., for constant help at every stage of the work. But none of these gentlemen are responsible for any defects in the work,

It would be failing in my duty if I do not mention the kind services of my friend Mr. Ramnath Goenka, M.L.C., in arranging with the Secretary and the members of the South Indian Humanitarian League, Madras, for the publication of this work.

I have to express my heartfelt thanks to Mr. C. Ramalinga Reddi, M.A., (Cantab), Vice-Chancellor of the Andhra University, for kindly accepting dedication of the work to that *Alma Mater* which is the crowning of glory afforded to Andhra renaissance, and which is a standing monument to his untiring zeal and effort.

THE COTTAGE,
MASULIPATAM,
1st October 1927.

L. L. SUNDARA RAM.

BIBLIOGRAPHY.

Bernier, Francois. Travels in the Mogul Empire. Translated by Archbald Constable. Second Edition revised by Vincent A. Smith. Oxford (1914).

Bhandarkar, D. R. Carmichael Lectures on Asoka. Calcutta University Press. (1925.)

Bhandarkar, (R.G.) Commemoration Volume. Bhandarkar Oriental Institute, Poona. (1917.)

Davies, Ainsworth, J. R. The Natural History of Animals. The Gresham Publishing House. London. Vol. VIII.

Dubois, Abbe. Hindu Manners, Customs and Ceremonies. Translated by Henry K. Beauchamp. Humphry Milford.

Dutt, Romesh Chunder. A History of Civilization in Ancient India. 2 Vols. Kegan Paul.

Encyclopaedia of Religion and Ethics. (E.R.E.) Edited by Henry Hastings.

Fick, Richard. Social Organisation in North-East India in Buddha's Time. Translated by Dr. S. K. Maitra, M.A., Ph. D., Calcutta University Press. (1920.)

Fuller, Sir Bampfylde. Studies in Indian Life and Sentiment. London. John Murray. (1910.)

Gandhi, Mahatma. Young India, 1919—1922. Madras. S. Ganesan, (1922.)

Gladwin, Francis. Ain-i-Akbari. (Translation.)

Gordon, Sir John. The Sikhs. William Blackwood, Edinburgh. (1904.)

Hoyland, J. S. Commentary of Father Monserrate. (Translation.) Edited with Introduction by S. N. Bannerje, Humphry Milford. (1922.)

Hume, Robert, A. An Interpretation of India's Religious History.

Ilbert, Sir Courtenay and Meston, Rt. Hon. Lord: The New Constitution of India, being three Rhodes Lectures by Sir Courtenay Ilbert and three by Rt. Hon. Lord Meston, delivered at the University College Session (1921-22) of the London University. University of London Press. (1923.)

Iyengar, Srinivasa, P. T. Life in India in the Age of the Mantras. Srinivasa Varadachar & Co., Madras.

Jee, Sir Baghavat Sinh. A Short History of Aryan Medical Science. Macmillan & Co. (1896.)

Keith, A. Berridale. Buddhist Philosophy in India and Ceylon. Oxford. (1223.)

Khadre, Gundu Rao. The Cow—My Dumb Mother. Manager, Sree Gorakshak Mandali, Bangalore.

Kipling, John Lockwood. Beast and Man in India, Macmillan & Co. (1892).

Law, N. N. Aspects of Ancient Indian Polity.

Levi, Sylvain. Doctrine du Sacrifice chez les Brhamanas.

Leyden and Erskine. Memoirs of Babar (Translation) 2 vols. Revised by Sir Lucas King. Oxford (1921.)

List, Frederich. The National System of Political Economy.

Macdonnel, Dr. A. A. A History of Ancient Sanskrit Literature. Macmillan & Co.

Masefield, John. The Travels of Marco Polo the Venetian (Translation). Everyman's Library. (1914.)

Mecauliffe, Max Arthur. The Sikh Religion. 6 Vols. Oxford, Clarendon Press. (1909.)

Monier-Williams, Sir Monier. Brahmanism and Hinduism. London. John Murray.

Mookerjee, Radhakumud. The Fundamental Unity of India. Longmans. (1914.)

Moreland, W. N. India at the Death of Akbar. Macmillan & Co. (1920.)

Morrison, Rev. Dr. John. New Ideas in India during the XIX Century. Macmillan & Co. (1907.)

Naoroji, Dadhabai. Poverty and Un-British Rule in India. London. Swan Sonnenschain.

Plato. The Republic. Translated by Jowett.

Rhys Davids. Buddhist India, T. Fisher Unwin. London. (1903.)

Rousseau, Jean Jaques. Contract Social.

Sacred Books of the Buddhists Series:—

Rhys Davids, Dialogues of the Buddha, Part I.

Rhys Davids, Mr. and Mrs. do. Part II.

Do. do. Part III.

Speyer, John S. The Jatakamala.

Sacred Books of the East Series :—

Bloomfield : Hymns of the Adharvaveda.
Buhler, Georg : Laws of Manu.
Buhler, Georg : Vasistha Dharmasastra.
Darmesteter, James : Zend-Avesta.
Eggeling, Julius : Satapata Brahmana.
Jolly, Julius : Institutes of Vishnu.
Oldenberg, Hermann : Vedic Hymns. 2 Vols.
Palmer, E. H. : The Qur-An.

Samaddar, J. Economic Condition in Ancient India. Calcutta University Press. (1922.)

Sarkar, Benoy Kumar : Sukraniti (Translation). Sacred Books of the Hindus Series. Panini Publishing House, Allahabad.

Sarkar, Jadunath. History of Aurangzib, 5 Vols. Rai M. C. Sarkar Bahadur, Calcutta.

Do. Mughal Administration, Readership Lectures of the Patna University.

Sen, Surendranath. Sivachchatrapati (Translation). Calcutta Univereity Press. (1920.)

Shamasastri, R. Ardhasastra of Kautilya. (Translation.). Madras, Wesleyan Press, 2nd Edition. (1923.)

Do. Evolution of Indian Polity. Calcutta University Press. (1920,)

Smith, Vincent, A. Early History of India. Oxford. (1914.)

Do. Oxford History of India. Oxford. (1920.)

Spencer, Herbert. Principles of Sociology. 3 Vols.

Stein, Sir Aurel. Kalhana's Rajatarangini. 2 Vols. Westminister, Archbald Constable. (1900.)

Syed Nazir Ahmed Saheb, Islami Gorakshan (Urdu.) Islami Gorakhan Office, Sitapur. (U.P.) (1925.)

Thurston, Edgar. Omens and Superstitions in South India.

Tytler, Alexandar Frazer. Considerations on the Present Political State in India. 2 Vols. London. (1815.)

Vaidya, C. V. History of Medieval Hindu India. 3 Vols. Aryabhushan Press, Poona.

Wadia, P. A., and Joshi, G. N. Wealth of India. London. Macmillan & Co. (1925.)

Williams, W. J. Hindu Theology, Vedic and Puranic. Calcutta. Thacker Spink. (1900.)

Wilson. H. Vishnu Purana. (Translation.) Haward Oriental Series.

Institution of Devadasis. By L. L. Sundara Ram. B.A. Indian Social Reformer, Vol. XXV, No. 47. July 25, 1925.

Cow-Killing. By Jaya Raja Rao. Ephiphany. Calcutta. Vol. XLII, No. 45. November 8, 1924.

Urea as a Diuretic in Advanced Heart Failure. By Drs. Crawford, Hamilton and McIntosh, The Antiseptic. Madras. Vol. XXIII, No. 3. March 1926.

Vaccination through the Mouth. Kalpaka. Vol. XXI, No. 4. April 26. 1926.

Corporation Slaughter Houses. M. Singaravelu. The Justice. Madras. 6th February 1926.

Beast and Man in India. By L. Moresby. The Jaina Gazette. Vol. XXI, No. 7. July 1925.

Race Characteristics of the Punjab. By Sir Michael O'Dwyer. A paper read before the Royal Society of Arts, (Indian Section), in February 1926.

Origin and Development of Sacrifice. By D. M. Sadiq. The Islamic Review. London. Vol. VIII, Nos. 6 & 7. June and July 1920.

Origin and Development of Sacrifices. By Dudley Wright. The Islamic Review. Vol. VIII, Nos. 8 & 9. August and September 1920.

Hindu and Muslim Unity. Presidential Address of Hakim, Ajmal Khan to the All-India Muslim League held at Amritsar in 1919.

Causes of Indian Disruption. By Savel Zimmend. New York Times Magazine. Reproduced in The Hindu. Madras. November 11, 1924.

Qurbani and Hindu Muslim Unity. By Hakim Ajmal Khan. Young India. Ahmadabad. June 7, 1920.

Cow Protection under Muslim Rule. By Dr. Syed Mahmud, Ph. D. Indian Review. Madras. August 1925.

Presidential Address of Maulana Mahomed Ali to the XXXVIII Sessions of the Indian National Congress held at Cocanada. 1923.

Shatrunjaya—where Hindus and Muslims pray in Union. Bombay Chronicle. Reproduced in The Muslim Outlook. Lahore April 8, 1926.

COW-PROTECTION IN INDIA

CHAPTER I.

INTRODUCTION.

IT may be stated without the fear of contradiction that of all the problems that are confronting the people of India at the present day, the problem of cow protection demands their earliest attention and sincere and genuine efforts to solve it. No doubt, India is now passing through an age of transition which is necessarily an age of national ferment. Political independence, economic regeneration, social reform, intellectual renaissance, communal still-waters and other allied problems are surging national activity. Each one of these problems demands our attention in no mean degree. But, behind all these, is discernible another far more important and all-comprehensive one, no less than the problem of cow-protection.

The bearings of the problem are far too many to be enumerated on one's fingers, while most of them overlap each other. Administration of forests, veterinary education and relief and tariff policy may, at first sight, seem to be quite exotic ideas to have any associatory value, much less an intimate connection, with the problem of cow-protection in India. Further it may seem to the layman that they are quite within the pale of the British Government of India, to have any reference to the activities of the body-politic. But, when once a proper diagnosis is made, and a breadth of vision and outlook is lent to him, he finds to his amazement what the nexus to the problem on hand to these sundry issues is like. The administration of the Indian forests and the rules relating to the access of the pastures available to the live-stock of the country is more a concern of the public than that of the Government, whatever may be the legal position of the red-tape and their control over them. It may be of small or no account to the Government if these pastures are led to develop and made available for public utility, as it is at the present day under the administration rules of the forests. What the Government is aiming at is an ample source of revenue and their attempts are directed towards successfully tapping them. We are not to question the *nature* of forest administration, but rest satisfied that this admirable source of income is only reducing the *per capita* levy paid by us into the coffers of the State towards its maintenance. But the public at large cannot afford to lose a moment in acquiring the last inch of the forest tracts that supply the natural grasses of the country and throw them open to cattle to feed upon.

Likewise, the policy of the Government as regards veterinary education and relief must not be entirely relegated to the polemics of the Governmental administrative policy of the country. Mere subsistence alone is not the be-all and the end-all of animal existence on earth. To live the life and live it with all the amenities, is something more than what is enjoyed at present by the cattle-world in India. To obtain that something, the indispensable desirability of which is established beyond doubt, we have to pre-suppose the existence of many elements that make life liveable. Besides food, immunity against pestilence, efficient and potent remedies in case of ailment, are essential to make the life of the animal tolerable. Immunisation and eradication are the two weapons in the hands of veterinary relief, and they must be diligently used both by the State and by the body-politic.

Again, take the question of the tariff policy of the Government of India. *Laissez faire* holds the field everywhere. The Government shows, in general, signs of indifference and apathy towards the growing industries of the country, though of late it is slowly making efforts to meet the legitimate aspirations of the people. Even though in several cases, cattle are slaughtered in large numbers solely for their carcases, Indians have a right to manufacture all the foot-wear necessary for indigenous consumption. If they cannot cope with internal demand, at least, they ought to have the possibilities of utilising all the hides and skins available in the country. This is not possible under modern economic conditions without the cover of an efficient tariff wall.[1] Industrial young India cannot withstand the onslaught of superiorly equipped countries which can dump their wares at such prices which can effectively oust the already struggling Indian industrialist from the economic market. But the Government is quite indifferent, and here it stands self-condemned. Large quantities of hides and skins are exported to foreign countries at un-imaginably cheap rates. At the same time, costly foot-wear

1. Cf. Frederich List: *The National System of Political Economy*. His arguments about young industries are commendable to any struggling nation.

is imported into the country. This does not simply mean a single loss. To kill cattle, especially live-stock, is an economic waste to an highly agricultural country like India. On the other hand, our industrial enterprise is crippled and rendered stagnant. Hides and skins are exported at a great loss, [1] and our hard-earned money is wasted on costly foot-wear bearing the stamp of British or foreign manufacture. The total loss can well be imagined. These and other allied problems will be dealt with elsewhere in greater detail. But to bring out the nexus of the problem of cow-protection to the political aspirations of the nation, these have been singled out for their homely impressiveness.

We say we do not have all these simply because the administrative policy of the Government is in the hands of an alien nation of domineering exploiters, while the Governmental machinery is absolutely rigid, [2] and unsympathetic towards Indian aspirations. When we recognise that the existence of these desiderata is due to the lack of popular hold on the deliberate actions of the mouth-piece of the body-politic, the nexus of the problem of cow-protection to the political aspirations of the country shines on the surface. And it is our duty to comprehend these problems and then try to solve them.

Next to the political side emerges the rationale connected with the economic activities of the body-politic towards the meticulous conservation of the bovine

1. Cf. W. H. Moreland: *India at the Death of Akbar*. London, Macmillan & Co., 1920, p. 163.

2. Cf. The late Mr Montague's remark: "The Government of India is rigid, wooden, iron, quite antediluvian to be of any practical importance at the present day."

species from extinction. The importance of the bovine species to national prosperity can in no way be discounted. No qualification seems to be necessary in pressing the practical application of the truth contained in the statement to any country, irrespective of the age and the economic potentialities circumscribing its material existence. The twentieth century needs the loan of an ample and efficient live-stock at least as much—if not more, but certainly not less, as the Paleolithic age that has gone two millennia before us. The bovine species is as much an indispensable and wholly desirable asset to a pre-eminently industrial country like America as it is to its very antipodes in the East noted for agriculture which is her staple industry. Agriculture, or more fittingly, the producing agent of the food-stuffs of the world and live stock go hand in hand. They are quite complementary. Each one is indispensable to the other. The efficiency of the one pre-supposes the hey-day of the other. Take away live-stock, there is no agriculture, and *vice versa.* The relativity of these phenomena is too obvious to need exposition in so many words. Hunger, the desire to fill up a vacuum in human want, exploits many means to achieve the end in view. Incommensurate quantity of food-stuffs would mean racial extinction. Agriculture is *the* industry that supplies the elemental needs of human existence. To promote agriculture, first of all build up an efficient agency of labour power. The chief animal agency which is within the reach of the ordinary man and which can supply the required motive-power to agriculture is the ox. Just as the medieval yeomanry supplied the pick of the armies in Europe, the ox is the main-stay of agriculture. Especially, the truth is literally applicable to the case of Indian agriculture. Organise your motive-forces, and conserve them from wanton and deliberate extinction. Preserve the traditional integrity which the cow used to enjoy at the hands of the Aryan race. Then alone India can produce the food-stuffs necessary to supply the stamina of her teeming population progressing at a geometrical ratio. Develop the breeds of the bulls, prevent them from the clutches of the butcher at a very tender age, sacrifice a vestige of the utilitarian spirit and thus contribute to national prosperity. If this is done, we shall have successfully gone through a major portion of our national ordeal. All this is anticipatory of our further investigations.

The intellectual, the moral and the sociological sides, come within the purview of an enquiry as to the place of the cow in the various theories of cosmology forwarded by the different religions that rose and fell in the annals of the world-history. Of all the influences that keep man inspired with a will to action, the influence of religion is the most considerable. Family affection and economic stress are simply transient goads in stabilising man's will to adhere to a particular dogma or pursue a distinct line of action. But the influence of religion,—the belief in the omnipotence of the Supernatural, acquires great potency in subjugating human volition to the dictates of inherent or acquired instincts relating to the perfect life on earth. Moral feelings, spiritual prepossessions, traditional view-points completely seize the imagination of mankind, more especially of the masses who form its majority. Simple belief in the tenets of the sacred books of a religion is sufficient to wrest from the populace all sense of rationality, and make it translate every word of the scriptures into action. Rationality and faith in religion may be taken as quite different poles. Whatever may be the encroachment at the present day of the rational spirit and critical judgment upon theology, especially of the so-called higher 'criticism' of the Protestant form of Christianity, it remains good always that the average man is but a willing instrument in the hands of religion. The promptings of religion are such that they lead man to blind-fold action irrespective of consequence. It is capable of making human beings *Ajivikas*, who are at once extreme fatalists and Huxleyan nihilists or it may lead them to the finest promptings of the *Sanatana Dharma*.

The communal tension between the Hindus and the Muhammadans in India at the present day about the sanctity of cow-life is an instance in point. Religion is capable of leading man to fanaticism. Concerted action can crumble empires. And if the Muhammadans still persist in killing cows invariably, whatever may have been the injunctions of the *Qur-An* and Arabic tradition, it is simply a vestige of the predominance of indiscreet sentimental dogmatism. Indeed, there is not even the slightest ordinance in the *Qur-An* about the indispensability of the cow for sacrificial purposes, as we shall see later on when we treat of the Muhammadan view-point. The practice of slaughtering cows is only a recent innovation wantonly embraced by the early Muhammadan invaders of India to taunt their Hindu subjects and find a ready justification for revelling in carnage and incendiarism during the subjugation of the provinces under the control of the Hindus, who naturally resent the least encroachment upon the life of the cow which they consider sacrosanct and inviolate, as will be plain from several anecdotes preserved in Sikh tradition. The present day communal riots in India owe their dynamite in one way to the conservation of the bovine species by the Hindus and the contrariwise bigotry of the Muhammadans. Nothing can go further in this respect than the recent *firman* of His Exalted Highness the Nizam of Hyderabad in penalising the possession of the picture of a cow by any subject in his dominions, declaring such possession to be criminal, punishable with a fine of Rs. 500 and a further award of six months' rigorous imprisonment in case the pictures are not surrendered one and all into the Tahsil Courts within a period of thirteen days of notification.[1]

With this real or assumed pride in the tenets of religion, and a cherished adherence to those divine ordinations, the masses are swayed in a great measure by popular superstition and general ignorance. Literacy in India has not attained any special degree of excellence. On the other hand, popular superstition rides roughshod over the intellectual capacities of the masses, which means a dark cloud hovering over the

1. An Associated Press of India message dated. Bombay, the 26th of April 1926 has the following announcement: " The Bombay Presidency Hindu Sabha is reliably informed that, on the 10th of April, His Exalted Highness the Nizam of Hyderabad issued an order by beat of drum, at Aurangabad, that thereafter it would be considered criminal to keep photos or pictures of a cow. 13 days from the date, all such copies of photos or pictures should be surrendered in the Tashil Courts of the Nizam and that after the said date, any person found in the possession of such a photo would be liable to a fine of Rs. 500 and six months' rigorous imprisonment."

prospective auguries of Indian literacy. According to the census of India in 1921, out of a total population of 318 412,480 the literate people number 22,623,651 of which 2,257,350 know English, which does not work up to 7 per cent.[1] Even of this seven per cent, the majority are steeped in ignorance, while their blind-fold views know no bounds. What is said in the sacred book, what is dictated by intuition and instinct must be done at once. The *pros* and *cons* of the problem are in no way to be judged. Once the impulse is given a start, there is an end of the matter.

In this respect, the materialistic west has contributed not an insignificant quota towards worsening the situation. I must not take slight notice of the incursions made by utilitarian philosophy on Indian culture. Bentham was individually a sagacious human being who has the power to "see the world steadily and see it whole". But his sagacity which is discernible in the exposition of his philosophy has been bartered by his later-day followers with fallacious theories that are evolved out of certain conditions which can be seen on the surface and are more apparent than real. One gentleman has advanced recently, [2] that to him, a prominent Hindu, there is no absolute quality of differ-

1. I compiled these figures from the *Statistical Abstract for British India* from 1911-12 to 1920-21. Parliamentary paper. Cmd. 2033. p. 28.

2. "To me, the cow is in no way superior to the goat or the pig, and a plea to save their innocent lives must be based only on humanitarian grounds. There are a very large number of Hindus who eat other meat than that of the cow. If the Hindus ask for indulgence from Muslims, owing to the former's religious susceptibilities, then there are the Jains in India whose religion

ence between a cow and a goat or a pig. If the killing of a pig or a goat is admissible, cow slaughter is to be admitted on equally like grounds. Even more. He contends, that the present output of food-

forbids them even to hurt a fly. Will those Hindus who are not vegetarians abstain from flesh food of all sorts in order to please the Jains? The Buddha taught mercy to all beings and practised vegetarianism himself. Are the present day followers of his creed vegetarians too?

The whole question is economic. Quoting your correspondent freely, the cow is an incarnation of Vishnu and as such is an object of worship. Hindus ought not to ill-treat the animal, but if the creature happens to be a particularly refractory incarnation, then its owner or keeper is justified in punishing it with a proviso of repenting afterwards. Agricultural produce, plus farmyard produce does not appear to provide enough food for the teeming population of the world in this industrial age, and flesh food supplies the deficiency. Returning to conditions in India, in particular, this is mainly an agricultural country and the people are pastoral. Methods of cultivation are still primitive as also means of traction, and the bullock and the cow play a very great part in India's life. What does the Hindu ryot or the dairy-man do when his cattle are no longer useful? He cannot afford to feed them when they have become unprofitable. Pinjrapoles are very few and the accommodation and the funds are totally inadequate to care for the enormous numbers of such old and weak animals that require protection. The bullock naturally goes to the hands of the butcher. The same fate awaits the cow. So long as she is young and wet she is truly cared for " like our mother without whose milk our life would have been impossible in childhood." But directly she becomes old and dry, the Hindu owner either directly or through a *chamar* negotiates with the nearest butcher for the sale of the " mother " doubtless with a view of expediting her further incarnations and renewing her usefulness to humanity. It is also beyond all doubt that the seller will "rue his conduct" after the transaction, or even perform "Go-bodh"! Who is to be blamed?" Mr. Jayaraja Rao of Cocanada in *The Epiphany*, November 8, 1924. Vol. XLII. No. 45. p. 179.

The deriding cynicism of these remarks is quite obvious. The average Hindu, for that matter, any human being will agree with me in pronouncing these statements to be quite unmoral, illogical and highly injurious to the national economy of any country in the world.

stuffs is quite insufficient to meet the demands on the part of the population of the world. The economic law of substitutes and complementary articles of food must find suitable food-material to fill up the gap. The existing number of sheep and goats is not sufficient to satisfy human hunger. The cow is the only fitting being on earth that can adequately fill in the abyss caused by human appetite. Hence, no difference between a cow and a goat or a pig. I need not comment upon the radicalism and short-mindedness of this line of argument.

Thus, the intellectual ebb of the masses, the indiscreet radicalism of the erratic, and a wholesome faith in the tenets of religion guide the masses in all their endeavours, including the economic. Of these, religious faith is the most salutary. Religious belief, faith, prepossession, or whatever you may call it, is one of the instincts coeval with the birth of civilization. It is an established thesis, that almost all the religions of the world are born in the infancy of modern civilization. After the genesis of the creed of the holy prophet Muhammad, in the seventh century of the Christian Era, practically there are no new propoundings of 'religion' in the larger sense. Whatever changes have taken place in the religious creeds of the world, are mere changes in doctrinal and superficial observances. The "higher criticism" of the more advanced section of the Protestants may quarrel about the historicity of the nativity of Jesus of Nazareth with its attendant superstitions, and the real import of the Last Supper. The Sanatanists and the Aryasamajists in India may plead for catholicity of outlook and equality of man in the face of God. Whatever changes there were, they were mere changes in interpretation, dynamic as contrasted with verbal, of the sacred texts. What changes there were, were mere purgings of undesirable elements that infect the original creed. The fundamentals always remain the same, but for the slight encroachment of popular superstition which is capable of doing harm in case it is pressed quite blindly and with the force of dogma, as the Muhammadan belief of the indispensability of the cow for sacrificial purposes on the *Bakra-Ki-Id* or *Bakra-Id* festival, as will be shown when we come to the Muhammadan view-point.

When we approach the nurseries of any religion, we find ourselves envisaging a glorious aspect of national economy meticulously conserved. Especially, the Indo-Iranian civilizations, and the religions which they brought into being offer us a consensus of opinion and outlook with other ancient civilizations as far as the promulgation of a guarded attitude towards the bovine species is concerned. One of the fundamentals of the religious economy, if I may use for the first time a strange combination of concepts, of the ancient civilizations, is the realisation of the indispensability of live-stock to national prosperity. Thus, in those ages of economic crudity and infancy of civilization, the wants of the people were few and simple. What they wanted were the mere elemental needs of human appetite,—sufficient food to eat and other amenities of human existence. Agriculture supplied their stock of food-stuffs, and flocks and herds their luxuries. A dish of cheese, a preparation of butter, a condiment of milk were all their caterers and served the purpose of what Shakespeare would call their "daintiest last". The collateral products of *ghee* were all the delicate niceties they could hanker after. Such is the medicinal value of milk and butter that they occupied a high place in Aryan hygiene; and the Vedic hymnal likens the appearance of God to *ghee*, [1] symbolically expressing its beneficial qualities. The bullock supplied the chief motive-power during their crude but arduous task of the exploitation of the soil and nature. With these antecedents and daily experiences it is no wonder that the early law-givers enjoined upon their believers a profound spirit of caution and reverence in their dealings with the cow. Beef-eating is under a sacred ban, while the cow and the bull are accorded niches in the altars of religion, litany and ritual.

The case of the other religions in India too is on a similar basis. As we shall see presently, even Muhammadanism is capable of expressing its appreciation of the benefits conferred by the cow upon humanity. As such, an inquiry into the sacrificial position of the cow must be made with a view to realise the exact attitude to cow-protection of the various religions in our country. This is absolutely essential in view of the fact that the stock plea of the religious implications of the slaughter of the cow at sacrificies will be of no fruitful account to the Muhammadan masses in India to make out a successful case for their present beliefs regarding cow-slaughter. On the other hand, frank admissions on our part, if any,

1. *Vedic Hymns*: part II. Translated by Hermann Oldenberg. iv. I, 6. S.B.E. Vol. XLII. p. 308.

of ancient Aryan practices of cow slaughter and the reasons for their subsequent abandonment must be made for a cogent reason. Especially when they are backed up by religious texts they will go a long way in making our Muhammadan neighbours pause a little and then endeavour to understand the bearings of the problem in their proper perspective with a view to see if they could possibly reconcile themselves to the feelings of their Hindu brethern.

If this is done the problem of cow-protection will no longer be the hegemony of the Hindus, as it is more an Indian problem than a Hindu one. The problem should never be relegated to the havoc of the devastating winds of communal bickerings. If it is done so, we will not be progressing even an inch and our communal problems, without solving which speaking of political freedom is madness,[1] will always remain with us. On the other hand, the problem must be realised to be of national rather than of sectional interest and concern. The various communities inhabiting India, including Muhammadans and Christians, are concerned in an equal measure with their neighbours the Hindus in evolving a solution to this most vexacious problem. Mere numerical superiority does in no way give the Hindu a right to monopolise the activities to protect the life of the cow. In fact, it will never succeed. On the other hand, the most genuine effort should be made to enlist the sympathy of our Muhammadan neighbours and thus secure their active and sincere co-operation. If facts and events are to be understood in their proper perspective and actual historical setting, it will be realised that the

1. Cf. Lord Meston's observations quoted in Chapter VII.

tug of war between the Hindus and the Muhammadans is mostly the product of the vindictiveness generated by several historical facts, such as a Muhammadan minority sovereignty over the vast majority of the Hindu population for many centuries, the acts of militant aggression on the part of the early Muhammadan conquerers of the Indian continent and the like. This will be fully realised when we see that not even a word of protest is being uttered against cow slaughter committed by the Europeans either in their houses or in cantonments.

Thus the best way to solve the problem of cow-protection in India would be to prepare a common meeting-ground for the Hindus and the Muhammadans alike. This could be done only by expounding on an authoritative basis that cow protective activity is not the monopoly and the special privilege of the Hindus, in as much as there is evidence to show that at one time in India cow-slaughter was prevalent, and that the Muhammadans have every concern with, and cannot fold their hands in indifference to, the problem, in view of the fact that besides there being no religious injunction or sanction of cow-slaughter for sacrificial purposes, most of our Muhammadan sovereigns have nerved themselves to protect cow-life. To do this an inquiry into the teachings of the various religions of India is essential, and this is attempted in the following pages.

CHAPTER II.

RELIGIOUS CODES AND THEIR SIGNIFICANCE.

THE sources of information about the social and religious beliefs of our ancient forefathers about the cow must be approached with great caution. It is a well-known fact to oriental scholars that the ancient Hindu *dharmasastras* and other sacred texts are often of an allegorical and symbolical character, losing much of precision, clarity and comprehensiveness in convenient platitudes.

Our ancient Hindu ancestors were religious to the core. As Dr. Hume put it: "The best illustration of the statement that man is 'incurably religious' is to be found in the Hindu people. 'Religion' influences their thought and action from before birth until after death. What made the Hindus such? God."[1] Not one act of their daily life is left untouched with a tinsel of religiosity. The prominent reason that accounts for this absolute and all-pervading garb of religion, or rather ritualistic and sacerdotal observances that clothes the mental attitude of the Aryans and their sons, the present-day Hindus, is to be found in the distinct sociological mould in which they were brought up generation after generation. A supreme conception of God, an exalted exertion towards the realisation of

1. *An Interpretation of India's Religious History.* By Dr. Robert A. Hume. p. 14.

Godly life on earth, a contingent discarding of all mundane trammels which are necessarily not of a high order, and a complete detachment from the ordinary functions of daily life—these are the special features of the general legacy bequeathed by the Aryan civilization and culture to the world. These features have such a romantic appearance as to completely capture the imagination of the man-in-the-street with an average intellect and they acquire a potency which will ultimately see to the willing acquiescence of the generality of the Hindu population. This is the reason why a marked difference is to be observable between the tone of the Hindu holy lore and the sacred texts of other nations in the world.

Another reason is to be found in the preponderating influence enjoyed by the Brahmanical priesthood who are, so to speak, the religious and moral sponsors of society and the practical dictators of civic action. In this respect, the Brahmanical priesthood offers excellent comparison to the Jewish heirarchy of Levites and Cohanim and the Parsee Magi of Media, who enjoyed more or less the same privileges as those enjoyed by their once-lucky brethren in the Far-East [1]. Such was the rigidity of social structure in ancient India, as it is even at the present day, that the Brahmans were compelled out of necessity to see that their influence maintains a steady good record of uniformity and does not in

1. Even though I am a Brahman, a Brahman, of the priestly class, after a careful examination of the holy texts, I am led to make these statements which may look a bit too radical to my brethren of the sacerdotal order. Here, it must not be forgotten that almost all our *dharmasastras* are the emanations of Brahmanical wisdom which has a unique history of its own and an uncompromising monopoly as well.

any way enter upon a career of waning due to the resenting and encroaching attempts of their so-called social inferiors.

Here I cannot refrain from quoting a significant passage bearing the impress of such a renowned scholar as Dr. Richard Fick, which brings out forcibly the one-sidedness and unnecessary drawn out phases of Brahmanical literature: "The time is past when people used to think that so far as ancient India was concerned, it was enough to consider only Brahmanical literature. The view that for ancient Indian culture and ancient Indian life we require only Brahmanical sources, is necessarily one-sided, because these sources were written from a onesided point of view. For their authors immersed in priestly views, the world which surrounded them, material as well as spiritual, existed only so far as they related to the sacrifices with their litany and their ritual which filled all their thoughts and aspirations and where, as in the text-books of law, there was a departure from this special view-point and the entire domain of law and morals for private as well of public life was taken into account, this was still done from the stand-point of theorising Brahmanism; nay, even in epic literature where one could expect most a view of the real state of things, this was prevented or, at any rate, rendered difficult, by the all-eclipsing underwood of theories and systems. No wonder that this world which the Brahmans interpreted in their own way appears so foreign and so strange to us: no wonder that in many points that it agrees so little with what we know of ancient India from other sides. Now-a-days, however, we no more consider a non-Brahmanical source, such as the accounts of the Greek messenger Megasthenes, unreliable simply because it cannot be brought into harmony with the Brahmanical theory; we try on the other hand, to collect all available material, whether it is of Buddhistic, Jaina, or Greek origin, which exhibits the priestly theories in their true light—nay, we do not even hesitate to make use of the conditions of modern India which on account of the stability of most Oriental cultures have preserved so much of the past for comparison with and for the explanation of earlier periods.

"Nowhere does the onesidedness of Brahmanical explanation seem so manifest as in the manner in which the Indian society is shaped in priestly literature. Heedless to all reference to facts, the Brahmans built up a theory which appeared to them to establish for ever through eternal and divine reasons, their rule" [1]. Even though Dr. Fick's statements refer to the fifth century B. C. and their relativity is limited to the *Jataka* stories and *Dharmic* texts we need not dispute the applicability of his statements to the Hindu sacred lore as a whole, divesting them of their local colouring and historical setting.

While compiling the *Dharma Sastras*, the *Smritis* and the *Srutis*, which are respectively the *heard* and *recollected* codifications of divine ordinations, and the *Brahmanas* and other compiled codes of sacrificial ritual, the Brahman is always to be seen as the officiating plenipotentiary of sociological phenomena. With him, the

1. *The Social Organisation in North-East India in Buddha's Time.* By: Dr. Richard Fick. Translated from the German by Dr. S. K. Maitra, M.A., Ph. D., University of Calcutta. 1920, pp. 1-3.

cow and the bull, symbols of purity and plenty, and energy and motive-power are exalted on earth. They are respectively the earthly embodiments of mental wisdom and material plenty which are always available for public service and general beneficence. With this line of thought as its basis, has been evolved a system of earthly deification of the Brahman and the cow. Willingly the other sections of the community, who are necessarily on a lower intellectual plane than their Brahman contemporaries, acquiesced in this convenient arrangement. [1]

But it is an observable fact, that whatever may have been the excessive privileges enjoyed by the Brahmans, it cannot be gainsaid that the *sastraic* and other sacred literature that emanated from their rich brains contained in themselves the concentrated essence of human wisdom handed down in strict lineal succession age after age down to the times when the codes were compiled. Neither can we discount the veracity and careful promulgation of sacerdotal observances by those super-men as they come down to us. But it is only a pardonable heresy if they erred on the side of an

(1) Categorical statements promulgating that the Brahman and the cow are earthly deities are not wanting in the Hindu sacred books. Cf *Satapata Brahmana.* "Verily there are two kinds of gods; for indeed, the gods are the gods; and the Brahmans who have studied and teach sacred lore are the human gods," Again, "Verily, there are two kinds of gods; for the gods themselves, assuredly, are gods; and those priests who have studied and teach Vedic lore, are the human gods." II, 2, 2. 6 and II, 4. 3, 14. S. B. E Vol. XII. pp. 309 and 374. Cf. Manu XI. 85. where it is stated that "a Brahman is an object of veneration even to the deities". Again, "mere birth itself confers divinity upon a Brahman". Manu. IX. 317; and even if he occupies the meanest of occupations, he must be honoured. *Ibid.* 319.

uncompromising monopoly of sacerdotal functions and exaggerated the position of the *dwijas* and *gomatas* on earth. And we would not be straying far from truth if we accept their statements as *bona fide* versions of actual social practices of those ages only varnished with some mixture of self-adulation. Such is the influence enjoyed by the priestly classes in ancient times that Plato the Greek philosopher recognised them as important personages in the personnel of governmental employees in his ideal state [1].

As regards the actual historical value of these records of ancient practices, which are more or less preserved at least in tradition down to the present day—and hence their practical usefulness, we cannot expect them as far as the position of the cow is concerned, to be quite static clearly expounding the theories and practices involved in their attitude towards the cow. Most of their observations are esoteric and highly symbolical, even though they are at times exoteric and categorical to the extreme, especially where they have to pronounce unequivocally the divine element in the *dwijas* and *gomatas*. As an instance in point, passages from the *Satapatha Brahmana* may be pointed to wherein specific statements are made about the Brahman being the earthly deity, and the cow being the incarnation of 'abundance' while being a highly deified image.[2] On

1. Plato: *Republic*.

2. See *Satapatha Brahmana*, II, 2, 2, 6; II, 4, 3, 14 and II, 3, 4, 27 respectively. Cf. Bloomfield: "As regards the Brahman, the overseer of the Srauta-performances, the Vait. Su. 1, 1, states that he must be conversant with the Brahma-veda, and in 1, 17, 18, this priest is described as *lord of beings*, lord of the world." *Hymns of the Atharva-Veda*, S. B. E. Vol. XLII. p. lix. The italics are mine.

the whole in our holy texts specific passages about the cow are few and far between, scattered over thousands of verses brought together in several ages and by several codifiers. It is therefore the task of the earnest student to cull them, place them in juxtaposition, churn them, assimilate them and finally offer a few statements summarily reviewing the nature of the position occupied by the cow in those ancient days.

To sum up, we have to approach the sacred books of the Hindus in the east with a great measure of caution. Besides their scattered nature, we are beset with the not-inconsiderable difficulty of skimming off all the glosses that are seen to be encrusting their statements. When this is done, we find ourselves in a position to draw a life-picture of those ages.

Likewise is the case with the sacred texts of other religions. Whatever religion or creed possessing a sacred text is taken into consideration, either Judaism, Christianity, Zoroastrianism, Buddhism, Muhammadanism and lately Sikhism, according to priority of birth, we find the influence of the priesthood always predominating. In fact, it will not be wrong if we maintain that the beliefs in the supernatural and the powers that be, and the methods of approach to them are respectively the emanations and workings of priestly intelligence. As such, writers of textual criticism on ancient codes conclude that many of them, religious and semi-religious, have undergone radical changes in the hands of their respective priest-hood, who either distorted or conveniently supplemented the teachings of their religious prophet or seer to suit the conditions of their earthly ministry. As an instance in point, the recent and laudable attempt of the members of the Bhandarkar Oriental Institute of Poona under the able guidance of Dr. V. S. Sukthankar to restore the original text of the *Mahabharata* may be mentioned.

But it has been asked several times, what is the practical import of these ancient religious codes at the present day? They are only suited to the early days of world civilization. Any attempt after the practical application of those *sastras* at the present day will be utopian and highly quixotic. Further, can they in any way rectify the already changing outlook of the Hindus towards the cow and her place in national endeavour? Is there even the slight degree of respect at the present day on the part of the Hindus towards those ancient *sastraic* compilations? A host of such questions have been piled up by unsympathetic critics against the utter inefficiency and unsuitability to the present-day atmosphere in India of the injunctions of the Hindu sacred lore of the past. They would point out that times have changed radically, that western materialisatic outlook has greatly warped India's social and religious atmosphere and,more than anything else, the economic motive is surging national endeavour. As regards the last named allegation, they would urge that a blind attempt to conserve kine-life is economically unwise, since the meat-eating sections of Indians are forced to buy mutton at a higher cost, in view of the fact that beef, though unimaginably cheaper than mutton, is put under the inexorable ban of social odium. But I will have occasion to show in another volume that the problem of the preservation of the bovine species is economically conducive to the nation's higher interests. Here it is only proper to tackle the original issue in detail.

No one can ignore the fact that the conditions obtaining in India have greatly changed since the ages when the Hindu *dharmasastras* and other codes of sacrificial ritual have been compiled. A process of social evolution, assimlation of exotic points of view consequent on centuries of foreign domination and indigenous subordination, and an imitation of the utilitarian West has rendered immeasurable harm to India at the present day. The development of the spirit of radical individualism and the consequent hey-day of individual critical acumen, whether good or perverted, conspired with the set of phenomena that have already given currency to exotic ideas as enumerated above. To aggravate and intensify the situation all the more, the economic motive coming to the forefront in modern times supplied an inventory of arguments, mostly erroneous and more apparent than real, and highly erratic, against the preservation of the bovine species. Poverty is endemic, and yet universally localised in India, to express the idea in terms of stern precision of logic ! [1]. The majority of the masses are being stared constantly in the face by the demon of hunger. Starvation. the economic Sword of Democles, is ever seen hanging over them. The quantity of food-stuffs in India is not sufficient to meet the growing demands of a teeming population ever increasing at geometrical progression. Whatever self-sufficiency India possessed in the days gone by, it has now been obliterated by

1. See the author's article on *The Institution of Devadasis. Indian Social Reformer.* Vol. XXXV. No. 47, July 25, 1925. p. 742.

foreign exploitation of her bumper crops. Governmental inaction as regards their tariff policy is highly instrumental in bringing about a set of economic conditions which are denuding the country of large quantities of food-stuffs that supply stamina to the Indian population. Side by side with this, there is the progressive deterioration of the soil consequent on its exhaustion by perpetual cultivation, insufficient and inefficient supply of manure and the incommensuarateness of live-stock to cultivate it. The degeneracy of the breeds, the inadequate supply of fodder and other leguminous plants to keep them up from exhaustion and ultimate decay, have not been rectified.

A host of causes like these, are rendering the position of the masses quite unbearable. Hence they make a virtue of necessity and in their moments of utter helplessness they lose all reason and far-sightedness and take to any new line of action suggested by half frantic and highly shallow utilitarians. Instead of straining their nerves to save themselves from falling into a worse plight, they render it all the more inense by their slipshod and misguided attempts to alleviate. In these attempts of theirs, they are subscribing themselves to what I may call an economic double impolicy. On the one hand the question of cattle improvement and the utter inadequacy of live-stock for agricultural purposes is demanding the strongest and most strenuous of national endeavours to rectify them. On the other hand, we find that even in highly industrial countries in the west, meat occupies only a minor part in satisfying human appetite. Take the case of England which is situated in the temperate zone and which requires a certain amount of heat-generating food. She is highly industrial and the annual output of crops and other food-stuffs is insignificant when compared with national demands. She is consequently forced to barter her manufactures for the food-stuffs of her colonies and other countries in the world, as she actually does at the present day. In such a special and most apt case as that of England, the consumption of meat does not come to any specially abnormal quantity. This is rendered so by the inadequacy of live-stock to the needs of the country. "It may be added that in June 1903, the total number of cattle in the United Kingdom amounted to 11,408,560, that is about 148 per thousand acres".[1] This is the case of a normal year in the pre-war days. During this decade and a quarter, with the geomatrical progression of population and the astounding development of utilitarian appetites, the supply of meat in the United Kingdom must indeed be still lower. Here we must not fail to take notice of the fact that England is more highly noted as a grazing, sheep-farming, and cattle-breeding country than as an agricultural one. With all her meat-supplying agencies, with all the regional qualities attendant on her physical configuration which demand certain heat-generating and highly invigorating food-stuffs, England is consuming a very insignificant quantity of meat. While it can be seen clearly that meat is not after all an indispensable article of human consumption over which nations have to rack their brains and improvise methods for raising a

---

1. *The Natural History of Animals.* By: J. R. Ainsworth-Davies. London. The Gresham Publishing House. Vol. VIII. p. 226.

plentiful supply of meat annually. On the other hand, the movement in England and other countries is of late more and more a policy of avoiding meat and taking to pure vegetarianism.

From this it is practically established that meat only plays a minor part in subserving human needs. Whereas, the case of India demands all the more acutely the disuse of meat-eating. Besides being highly unsuited to the conditions of life under a tropical sun, meat-eating involves a high toll upon the animal life of agricultural India which depends mainly upon the labour power of the live-stock, and hence detrimental to national interests. All the while the connotation of the word 'meat' is not restricted to the emoluments of the flayed carcases of sheep and goat. When the specific item of preserving bovine life from extinction comes within our purview, we cannot fail to take cognizance of the fundamental importance of their preservation. In this way it is manifest that the radicals who are advocating an open policy of free-trade and non-intervention specially in respect of the bovine species, are committing an economic double impolicy which is at once derogatory to national traditions and historical legacies, and suicidal to national prosperity.

This unwonted and unwise departure from India's traditional conservatism and sacred preservation of kine-life, and the economic fallacies of this radical double-impolicy of the present day bring forth in clear perspective the importance of the *Dharmasastras* at the present moment in catering to national interests. It is not simply a question of national reconstruction on the basis of bye-gone traditions ; it is not simply a movement towards the vindication of the excellences of Aryan culture and Aryan civilization ; it is not simply a desire to pride in Indian traditions as such, that add further support towards accepting many of the desirable elements in our ancient sacred codifications. It is, on the other hand, the imperative necessity on the part of the Indians to once again trace their steps back to the several salutory practices of the Aryans from which they are led to stray away partly by their innate misdirected judgment and partly by the proselytising influences for the worse of a long period of alien suzerainty. Especially the Hindu practices of preserving cow-life, the improvising of enough room around every habitat for purposes of pasturage, as will be shown in fuller detail subsequently, must be followed with great precision. This renders it imperative on our part to make a guarded approach to the ancient Hindu codifications.

Besides all these disturbing elements, there is the undeniable presence of Aryan culture in our present-day national endeavour. Edward Freeman was never tired of reiterating the immortal truth about the fundamental unity of history. The present is only the outcome of the past, the fruition of the genuine endeavours on the part of the people that have gone before us. We are not the products of our own individual endeavours merely, either. We have our own legacies bequeathed to us by our ancestors. We have our own traditional outlook towards life handed down to us from generation to generation. We have our own individual national aspirations and national endeavours. We have, in short, a distinct sociological mould meticulously preserved by our inherent conservatism, in which our ideas take shape and our actions crystallise. The case of Aryan civilization is unique in the chequered history of the world. Civilizations have had their own day and have disappeared like meteors. Nations rose and fell with their local historical settings. Rome was able to inundate the Teutonic institutions in the west. Christianity accomplished momentous revolutions during the middle ages, but the Aryan Civilization, tracing its genesis back to two or three thousand B. C., or even to four thousand B. C., in the light of the recent excavations and finds of the Archaelogical Department of India at Mahanjo Daro and Harappa, enjoys a unique history during all the storms of alien intrusion and national sub-ordination. Everything that exists in India is distinctly Aryan, and when I make this statement, I am not far from expressing actual truth. The extant monuments of Aryan Civilization, especially of the archaeological section, speak for themselves, a recollection of which will churn the sentiment of every true-born Indian and fill his heart with the ecstatic thrill of our historic past. Dr. Radhakumud Mookerjee is prominent among scholars in pointing out the fundamental unity of India, [1] and even western scholars like the late lamented Dr. Vincent A. Smith who are noted for their conservatism have lost no time in conceding this fundamental trait of our national character. "India, beyond all doubt, possesses a deep underlying fundamental unity, far more profound than that produced by either geographical isolation or by political suzerainty. That unity transcends the innumerable diversities of blood, colour, language, dress,

1. *The Fundamental Unity of India.* By Radhakumud Mookerjee. Longmans. 1914.

manners, and sect."[1] We have preserved our civilization as handed down to us by our Aryan ancestors. We have the unique distinction of having clung to our *Sanatana Dharma* which alone accounts for the peaceful relationship maintained by the Hindus with the different religions that have found a place in India and given her the appellation of the 'emporium of religions' The Hindu religious policy of non-intervention and letting every person alone to realise the consummation of his mission on earth and become merged in the Supreme *Atman* has a distinct advantage over other religions and pleads for universal adaptability. With the practical suitability of Hindu religion to every age come to the surface the best qualities of our *Dharmasastras* in which are embedded the cardinal principles of Hinduism. There they stand with all their lusture and pristine glory, and it is only up to us to partake of the light to the best of our capacity and to the extent of our necessity. When this is done, we need not fear any extraneous and undesirable elements thwarting our endeavours and besetting our paths, but find a useful solvent of such grave problems.

One more point presses itself on our attention in this respect. It is the retrospective effect upon the the present generation of the contemplative attitude towards the sacred lore of a religion. The firm imprint of evolution is always observable in the history of any nation. In matters concerning religion, its importance is all the more real. The religion of the present is the supreme heritage of the past. Every religion is

1. Vincent A. Smith: *The Oxford History of India*, p. x. Oxford. Clarendon Press. 1920,

initially a revolt against the pre-existing undesirable elements in the attitude of a people towards God, man and nature. A prophet or incarnation springs up, proves a radical as far as the then existing beliefs are concerned, and formulates the doctrinnaire of his own creed. Through the process of ages the creed makes accommodation for modulating tendencies to suit changing conditions. To understand perfectly the present stand of a religion, its past history must first be studied. As M. Darmesteter puts it: "No language, no religion that has lived long and changed much, can be understood at any moment of its development unless we know what it was before and what it became afterwards".[1] Again, with an even ampler measure of truth and veracity, he says: "Any living people, although its existing state of mind is but the result of various and changing states through many successive stages, yet, at any particular moment of its life, keeps the remains of its former stages in order, under the control of the principle that is then predominant."[2]

That the past has its indelible impression upon the present is established beyond doubt. More important is the point, that a realisation of this fundamental fact as forcibly expressed by M. Darmesteter will have its rich effects upon any living nation. Especially, when any nation shows signs of decadance due to the development of a certain spirit of apathy towards, and negligence of

1. *The Zend-Avesta*: Translated by James Darmesteter, S. B. E. Vol. IV. part I. The Vendidad, Introduction, p. xxix. (1895.)

2. *Ibid.* p. xxx.

the past, which leads to social stagnation, as is the case with the present-day India, the contemplation of the sacred lore of the past offers a strong corrective to the present. Ignorance of the *Dharmasastras* of the Aryan past, misuse or non-use for centuries of Aryan practices, and consequent small-mindedness of the population has done great harm to India. It is a pity that western scholars of various nationalities have to unearth the long-forgotten lore of India, and show us the proper paths of appreciation of our *Dharmasastras*. When once this particular spirit is cultivated, national aspirations will have been achieved. This is wanting in the India of the present-day, which is only making a faint effort in this respect. Perhaps, it would not be long before she enters upon this brilliant phase of patriotic endeavour.

CHAPTER III.

THE HINDU ATTITUDE.

"THE cow is one of the greatest blessings to the human race. No nation or people has become highly civilized without her. She produces the best human food on earth. She makes this health-building, strength-giving food from grass and coarse plants. She provides not only for the young and her keeper's family but also a surplus to sell. Where cows are kept and cared for, civilization advances, lands grow richer, homes grow better, and debts grow fewer. Truly the cow is the mother of prosperity." This naive description by Mr. A. Hayne of Chicago [1] of the benefits conferred by the cow upon human civilization fits in exactly with our exposition of the profound feelings of our Aryan ancestors about the cow which ultimately led to its deification.

The early domestication of the cow has left an indelible impression upon Indian life and thought. When the civilization of the world was anything but remarkable, when the legacies of the Egyptian and Assyrian cultures were relegated to the back-ground, when barbarism was flourishing as in a hot-bed, the Aryan peasantry, with their pastoral and agricultural excellence, with their knowledge of civilized arts and crafts, with their superior and marvellous mental equipment which produced the best of ancient thought and wisdom, dazzled the world in an exceptionally remarkable degree. One of the prominent features of their social superiority was the realisation and recognition of

---

1. *Indian Review*. Dec. 1924. quoting the article of Mr. W. H. Harrison, Agricultural Adviser to the Government of India, in the *Statesman*, Calcutta.

the fundamental importance of agriculture to the body-politic, and more especially of cattle requirements to make that needed agriculture thrive.

This recognition on their part of the absolute requisiteness of live-stock for social purposes made them conserve cattle life, especially of the bovine species, with meticulous care. This is evident from their invocations to Varuna and Mithra to shower plenty of rain and make their cattle thrive. Dr. Kaegi admirably sums this up in the following manner: [1] "The principal means of sustenance was cattle keeping. Repeatedly in the hymns we meet with the prayers for whole herds of cows and horses, sheep and goats, heifers and buffaloes, but *especially of milch-cows*, which are, to more than one singer, the sum of 'all good which Indra has created for our enjoyment'. But by divine power, the red cow yields the white milk from which is prepared mead and butter, the favourite food of gods and men, and perhaps also cheese" With this recognition of the importance of cattle and the careful protection of cattle-wealth by the ancient Aryans, emerges to the surface the supreme importance and exaltedness of the cow in their view.

Before entering upon the various theories of cosmology propounded by Aryan wisdom and the place of the cow in them, it is but proper and instructive to investigate the economic environs of the Aryan society and the place of the cow in the working exposition of their economic endeavours. This is particularly required for one cogent reason. Society and social wisdom are inordinately influenced by the prevailing economic structure of a particular age. Especially in the case of

1. *The Rigveda*, p. 13. The italics are mine.

a civilization which was in its infancy this influence is all the more operative, since literature may almost be said to be non-existent, religious texts not as yet codified, and social wisdom not crystallised into definite form. Above all, the predominant influence exercised by agriculture and cattle-wealth absorbed the mental outlook of the Aryans. When literature, secular and religious, was in the making, in such an age, the existing economic conditions which were, after all, matters of daily observance are sure to operate strongly upon the minds of the early codifiers of sacred texts in their efforts to create systematic literature. Such is the spectacle we visualise in the writings of early Roman poets. [1] And we find this revealed in a large measure in the literature of the Vedic and the post-Vedic periods which are at once copious and vivid. An examination of this phenomenon will be of great use to us in our efforts to work out and understand the various theories of cosmology evolved by the Aryans in relation to the existence of the cow on earth.

---

1. Cf. Dryden's Virgil. *Georgics* Bk. III.

"The *mother cow* must wear a lowering look,
Sour-headed, strongly-neck'd to bear the yoke;
Her double dewlap from her chin descends,
And at her thighs the ponderous burden ends.
Long as her sides and large, her limbs are great;
Rough are her ears, and broad her horny feet.
Her colour shining black, but fleck'd with white;
She tosses from the yoke: provokes the fight.
She rises in her gait, is free from fears,
And in her face a bull's resemblance bears:
Her ample forehead with a star is crown'd
And with her length of tail she sweeps the ground.
Lofty-neck'd;
Sharp-headed, barrel-belly'd, broadly back'd,
Brawny his chest and deep."

I am obliged to my friend Mr. H. M. Douglas for this reference.

Prof : Samaddar gives a comprehensive survey of the economic position of the cow in the light of Aryan wisdom in his *Economic Condition of Ancient India.*[1] He says: "Kine, even then was very likely the medium of exchange, signifying certainly a primitive stage of society. The price of a particular cow is mentioned in terms of kine. Indeed, in almost all the passages which I am able to collect, though silver and gold are mentioned, and I take it that these are generally silver and gold coins, importance has been invariably given to kine. King Dasaradha does give gold and silver but does it along with ten lacs of kine. When the king gives away the four quarters of the world to the sacrificial priests, they wanted as the price thereof gems and gold but preferably kine. The king is indeed spoken of as dispensing *dakshinas* profusely, but he does it along with hundreds and thousands of kine. His daughter-in-law, the inimitable Sita, also evidently attached more importance to kine than to gold and silver, for in addressing the Ganges as well as Kalindi to propitiate them, she promises to offer thousands of kine. Certainly, if she had liked, and if gold and silver had been the general medium of exchange, she would not have laid particular importance to the kine. We are told again, that the banks of Gomati were filled with kine. When Rama was giving away his wealth, he rewards the Brahman Trijata with cows and bullocks though we find him giving away gold coins as well." Eventhough Prof : Samaddar is referring here to the economic aspect of Indian life as can be gleaned from the stray verses of

1. Chapter III. "Ramayana from the Economic point." pp. 69-70. Calcutta University Press. 1922.

the Ramayana, there is no gainsaying the fact that the economic conditions obtaining in the pre- and post-Ramayana ages show us the same phenomenon wherein the cow is to be seen as a medium of barter besides being a measure of value. But Prof: Samaddar's commitment that Sita would have promised to propitiate the Ganges and the Kalindi with gold and silver, if these metals were used as media of exchange instead of with kine, is open to qualification. We cannot say categorically that gold and silver were totally unknown as media of exchange to the people of the Ramayana period. But the possible reason for the inimitable Sita to prefer kine to these metals is to be sought in the religious sanctity of the cow coupled with its economic importance in subserving human ends.

The importance of agriculture and pasture figure more prominently in the ages past, than it does at the present day in the national economy of India, thus adding further strength to the value of cattle life especially of the bovine order. According to Sukra,[1] the cow is included among the components of an ideal house-hold. Hymn 19 of Book X of the *Rig Veda* is an instance in point: "We call thee cowherd, let him take out these cows; let him pasture them in the fields; let him bring them back to the house; he pastures them on all sides. May he come home safe! O cowherd! pasture the cows in all directions and bring them back. Pasture them in various parts of the earth and bring them back." Commenting upon this memorable verse,

1. *Sukraniti.* III. 481-2. Translated by Benoy Kumar Sarkar, Sacred Books of the Hindus series.

Mr. Romesh Chandra Dutt remarks,[1] "that we shall seek in vain in the entire range of Sanskrit literature for a passage in which the humble hopes and wishes of simple agriculturists are so naturally depicted."

Even more emphatic passages are those supplied by the hymnal of the *Adharva Veda*. There are several *charms* in the form of prayers by the Aryan votary taken recourse to to attain his cherished ends.[2] There is a charm for the prosperity of cattle.[3] The Aryan votary invokes Vayu, Savitar, Brihaspati, Ammavati and the whole band of beneficent supernaturals to keep their flocks together and safely conduct them home on their return from pastures. "I pour together the milk of the cows, I pour together strength and sap with the ghee. Poured together shall be our herds, constant shall be the cows with the owner of the cows. I have brought hither the sap of the grain. Brought hither are our heroes, brought hither to this house are our wives". The intensity of the love towards the cow generated by individual instinct and the economic contribution of the cow to human well-being are most sincerely reflected in this passage. In another passage[4], the same theme is harped upon with characteristic eloquence. It invokes godly help to unite the flocks of cattle and lead them to the stables of the owner. It prays for the prosperity of

1. *A History of Civilization in Ancient India*, p. 40.

2. *Hymns of the Adharva Veda*, II. 21.1-5 ; III. 14. 1-6; *V*. 18, 1-15; VI. 59. 1-3 ; VI. 70. These are only a selection of the most important *charms* which are relevant to our present purpose. S. B. E. Vol. XLII. Bloomfield.

3. *Ibid.* II. 21. 1-5.

4. *Ibid.* III. 14. 1-6.

the cows and the plenty of their seed and their faithfulness to their owner. "Right here come, ye cows, and prosper here like the *Saka*-bird ! And right here do ye beget (your young) ! May you be in accord with me !..... Attach yourselves O! cows, to me as your possessor; may this stable here cause you to prosper ! Upon you, growing humorous and living, may we, increasing in wealth, alive, attend!". The last sentence is the crowning of affection afforded to the cow by the Aryans. Another hymn [1] invokes Arundhati to empty the horn of plenty upon the Aryan stables and protect the cows when on pastures. Hymn VI. 70. embodies a charm to secure attachment of a cow to her calf.

Besides these positive invocations, the hymnal of the *Adharva Veda* contain many passages wherein cow-killing is deprecated as the most heinous of crimes. Hymn V. 18 of the *Adharva Veda* is a standing condemnation of any encroachment on the life of the cow. Under pain of moral damnation, the cow cannot be slaughtered. The Aryan agriculturist fills the atmosphere with importunities against the killing of cows and this hymn reveals it in a striking manner. "Enveloped (is she) in her skin as an adder with evil poison ; do not, O ! prince (eat the cow) of the Brahmana ; sapless, unfit to be eaten is that cow." (v. 3). In a later verse (v. 11) he threatens the perpetrator of the crime with vindictive Nemesis and sings : "The cow hereself, when slaughtered comes down upon the Vaithavyas who had roasted for themselves the last she-goat of Kesari-prabhanda ".

1. *Ibid.* VI. 59. 1-3.

According to Manu,[1] cow-killing is an *Upapataka*, and the Hindu law according to Vasistha[2] inflicts a *Taptakrikhkhara* penance upon the perpetrator of the crime dressed in the raw hide of the cow if that culprit chanced to be a Brahman. According to that familiar verse of the *Mahabharata*[3] "all that kill, eat and permit the slaughter of cows rot in hell for as many years as there are hairs on the body of the cow slain". Capital punishment was inflicted on those who either steal, hurt or kill a cow or abet others to do so, and Kautilya lays down[4]: "Whoever hurts or causes another to hurt, or steal or causes another to steal, a cow, should be slain".

The Aryans further rationalised the condemnation of beef-eating in a strikingly plausible manner. Rev. Dr. John Morrison describes this in the following passage.[5] "To kill a cow is as bad as to kill many men. For, suppose a cow to have a lifetime of fourteen or fifteen years. Her calves, let us say, six cow-calves and six bull-calves. The milk of the cow and her six cow-calves during her natural life time would give food for a day to an army of 15,440 men according to the founder of the Aryas, while the labour of the other six calves as oxen would give a full meal to an army of 256,000 men. Therefore, to kill a cow etc. Q. E. D." Eventhough we

1. *Institutes of Manu.* XI. 60.

2. *Vasistha Dharmasastra.* XXI. 23. S.B.E. Vol. XIV. p. 113.

3. *Ibid.* XIII. 74. 4

4. *Arthasastra.* Book III. ch. xxix. Translated by Dr. R. Shamasastri. 2nd. Edition. (1923).

5. *New Ideas in India During the XIX Century.* p. 116. By Rev. John Morrison. M.A., D.D., Macmillan, (1907).

may not be in a position to accept literally this rationalisation of the Aryans, we can readily discern the element of truth contained in it, that to deplete the country of bovine cattle would mean the sure starvation of her sons in a greater or a lesser degree.

Instances of this kind may be multiplied to any extent. But it is sufficient to note the fundamental point that our Aryan ancestors have clung passionately to the recognition of the importance of the cow in the national economy of India. And we may note here that they are totally undeceived in asserting their conviction as we, who live in the XX century, do find ourselves envisaging the same set of truths as those which our ancestors experienced before us.

One important fact is to be taken cognizance of before we proceed to work out the positive theories of cosmology and the place of the cow in them according to the various systems of Hindu thought. We cannot afford to be ignorant of the fact that at one time Aryans used to consider cows as fit objects for a sacrificial holocaust. And it is a delightful spectacle for us to imagine the early Aryans passing from darkness to light, from an once-convenient practice to a reasoned and highly beneficial dogma, from deeming bovine cattle as fit offerings to supply the amentum to the gods they adored to declaring them sacrosanct. The reasons for the vogue of such a practice and its subsequent abandonment are to be sought in the fact that the Aryans—accepting the most popular theory of their migrations, were not so strongly impressed with the importance of cows to the community while they were making away from their abode in mid-Asiatic steppes. The bounteous tracts of the land watered by the Five Rivers might have served the purpose of an eye-opener in making them realise their folly in denuding the country of a potential source of prosperity such as the bovine cattle supply to agricultural India. This suggestion is proved in a measure by the theory of the evolution of practices as regards the selection of animal victims at sacrifices, fully expounded in the *Satapatha Brahmana* [1] wherein the sacrificial victim changes from a man to a goat passing through the intermediary stage of the cow. This we will see in greater detail later on, but here we will stop for supplying evidence to estabish the point that cows were once thought to be fit offerings at a Brahmanical sacrifice.

For one thing, Manu ordinances : [2] " For the sustenance of the vital spirit, Brahma created all this animal and vegetable system; and all that is moveable and immoveable, that spirit devours." This would make man the supreme master over the living world and he can use his discretion in discriminating between lawful and unlawful food ; as the Muhammadans, as we shall see in a subsequent chapter, are wont to lay special stress upon. This is in quite easy agreement with that verse of the Bible [3] which says : " And God said, let us make man in our own image, after our likeness ; and let him have dominion over the fish of the sea, and over the fowl of the air, and over the cattle and over all the earth and

1. I. 2. 3. 6.
2. *Institutes of Manu.* v. 28.
3. *The Holy Bible, Genesis.* I. 20. (Authorised Version).

over every creeping thing that creeps upon the earth." And it is lawful for him to partake freely of all sources of food, vegetable as well as animal.

Manu is even more explicit in this respect in laying down that whatever is offered first in sacrifice and then taken is perfectly lawful food. [1] The flesh of the animal must only be hallowed with the repetition of *mantras* before it is taken in, [2] so that it might become lawful food ; and the man, especially a Brahman, who refuses to partake of the emoluments of the consecrated animal would sink in another world for twenty-one births to the state of a beast. [3] But under no circumstances, Manu warns us, shall there be any wanton indulgence in the slaughter of animals. [4]

When we attempt to have a clear idea of the nature of Aryan sacrifices with special reference to bovine cattle, we find in early Hindu literature sufficient information to establish the thesis that cows were once victimised at sacrifices and used at times as articles of food. Meat eating was at one time universal in India and cows were sacrificed, and at *sraddhas* "the aroma of beef was thought to be an excellent aliment for the spirits". [5] According to a queer Vedic practice,[6] it is plain that animals, generally goats, were sacrificed before the cremation ceremony of a corpse was proceeded with, and

1. *Institues of Manu.* V. 32-37.
2. *Ibid.* V. 36.
3. *Ibid.* V. 35.
4. *Ibid.* V. 37.
5. *Brahmanism and Hinduism.* p. 194. By Sir Monier-Williams.
6. *Adharva Veda.* IX. 5. 1-3.

there is ample evidence to maintain that cows too were offered up to the gods before the decaying entrails of the human body were consumed by the flames of the crematorium.[1] Even the *Rig Veda* leads us to subscribe to the theory of the prevelance of the practice of cow-slaughter in ancient *Aryavarta.*[2] In *Uttara Rama Charitra* we find Valmiki regaling Vasistha with the "fatted calf" which surely leads us to the fact that at one time in Indian History beef-eating was not uncommon. We are told in *Vasistha Dharmasastra*[3] that it was declared by Vagasaneyaka that the flesh of milch cows and oxen is fit for sacrifices. Yajnavalkya is declared to have said:[4] "I, for one, eat it (beef), provided it is tender". The *Grihya Sutras* permit the slaughter of a cow on the arrival of a guest, especially at a wedding or a sacrifice.[5] From *Satapatha Brahmana* I. 2. 3. 6 it is certain that it is a reference to the once-prevalent practice of sacrificing bovine cattle for ritualistic purposes.

Post-Vedic and Buddhist literature offer us ample material in this respect. Especially, the Buddhist canon, which we will countenance fully in the next chapter, is a standing condemnation of the Aryan type of sacrifice wherein no hesitation was once shown as regards the slaughter of bovine cattle. For our present

1. *A History of Ancient Sanskrit Literature.* p. 125. by Dr. A. A. Macdonnel.

2. *Ibid.* p. 149.

3. XIV. 46. S.B.E. Vol. XIV. p. 74. Translated by Dr. Georg Buhler.

4. *Satapatha Brahmana.* III. 1. 2. 21.

5. See Jacobi: *Encyclopaedia of Religion and Ethics.* Vol. IV. pp. 224—226. Art. Cow (Hindu).

purposes, that significant passage from the *Kutadanta Sutta*[1] is sufficient witness to this set of phenomena wherein it is mentioned that Gotama prevented the Brahman Kutadanta from performing a sacrifice with "*a hundred bulls*, and a hundred steers, and *a hundred heifers*, and a hundred goats and a hundred rams [which] had been brought to the post for sacrifice."

From the cumulative evidence which has been so far gathered it is practically established that cow-slaughter was known to the Aryan communities of the ages past and that it was a later-day development of Aryan sentiment to deem cows as sacrosanct and damn cow-slaughter as a deicide. The result is the outcome of the lessons of experience and the steady observation by the Aryans of the benefits conferred by the cow on the agricultural population of India.

The transition from slaughtering cows at sacrificial occasions to a total ban on beef-eating and deeming cows as sacrosanct is a process of ages and has for its basis the focus of the influence of several sociological associations. On the one side, there is the realisation of the importance of bovine cattle to agricultural purposes and a faint foreboding that the allowing of cow slaughter would lead to the ultimate denuding of the country of live-stock. There is the recognition of the extreme usefulness of the products of the cow which add in not an inconsiderable degree to the stamina of the

1. *Dialogues of the Buddha.* Part I. p 174. Sacred Books of the Buddhists Series. Vol. II. Translated by Rhys Davids. Oxford. Humphry Milford. (1923).

The italics are mine.

human world, as can be seen from several poetic conceits and hyperboles showered upon the cow. [1] There is the evolutionary process in the selection of the animal victim, descending from the highest (human) to the lowest (goat), so well described in *Satapatha Brahmana*,[2] and finally the total abstention from killing animals at all but invoking the animal victim into the specially prepared cake of dough offered at sacrifices. [3] There are the promptings of the humanitarian instinct of man which forbids all kinds of infliction of cruelty on living creatures, under pain of damnation, much less of slaughtering a creature like the cow which has a physiological organism that can feel the torture and make the standers-by visualise it. Buddhism had played an important part in bringing about this evolution, or revolution, as you may call it, in the abandonment of animal sacrificies in general and cow-sacrifices in particular. Speaking of the story in the *Kutadanta Sutta*, which we shall relate in the next chapter, Dr. Rhys Davids opines [4] that "the Vedic sacrifices of animals had practically been given up when the long struggle

1. See *Encyclopaedia of Religion and Ethics*. Vol. IV. p. 224. Dr. Jacobi mentions that the word *go* which originally denotes 'cow' is given as synonym of earth, heaven, rays of light, speech, and singer, in fact any highly valuable thing, or any thing which has a dignity of a very high order. Cf. *Institutes of Vishnu* IV. 1-6. "Like the bright heated butter of the cow (the appearance) of the God is lovely, like the bountifulness of a milch cow."; or III. 17-1 where it is described that Agni's robe is ghee'. Nothing can go beyond this verse in point of attachment to and general praise of the qualities of the cow.

2. I. 2, 3, 6.

3. *Ibid.* I. 2, 3, 5. and *Rajatarangini*. III. 7, Stein Vol. I. p. 72.

4. *Dialogues of the Buddha*. Part I. p. 165. Translated by T. W. Rhys Davids. Sacred Books of the Buddhists. Vol. II.

between Brahmanism and Buddhism reached its close. Isolated instances of such sacrifices are known even down to the Muhammadan invasion. But the battle was really won by the Buddhists and their allies, and the combined ridicule and earnestness of our Sutta will have had its share in bringing about the victory." All these causes conspired together in bringing about a gradual change in the selection of the animal victim, ultimately putting a total ban on cow-slaughter at sacrifices, much less on ordinary occasions.

The theory of evolution in the selection of the animal victim fully described in the *Satapatha Brahmana*,[1] is to be noted with interest. " At first, namely, the gods offered up a man as the victim. When he was offered up the sacrificial essence went out of him It entered into the horse. They offered up the horse, when it was offered up, the sacrificial essence went out of it. It entered into the ox. They offered up the ox. When it was offered up, the sacrificial essence went out of it. It entered into the sheep. They offered up the sheep. When it was offered up, the sacrificial essence went out of it. It entered into the goat. They offered up the goat. When it was offered up, the sacrificial essence went out of it.

" It entered into this earth. They searched for it, by digging. They found it (in the shape of) those two (substances), the rice and barley; therefore, even now they obtain those two by digging; and as much efficacy as all those sacrificial animal victims would have for

1. I. 2. 3. 6-9.

him, so much efficiency has this oblation (of rice etc,) for him who knows this. And thus there is in this oblation that completeness which they call 'the five-fold animal sacrifice'.

"When it (the rice-cake) still consists of the rice-meal, it is the hair. When he pours water on it, it becomes flesh: for then it becomes consistent; and consistent also is flesh. When it is baked it becomes bone: for then it becomes somewhat hard; and hard is the bone. And when he is about to take it off (the fire) and sprinkles it with butter, he changes it into marrow This is the completeness which they call 'the five-fold animal sacrifice'.

"The man (*purusha*) when they offered up became a mock-man (*kim-purusha*). Those two, the horse and the ox, which they had sacrificed became *Bos Gaurus* and a *Gayal* (*Bos Gavaeus*) respectively. The sheep which they sacrificed, became a camel. The goat which they offered became a sarabha. For this reason one should not eat the flesh of these animals, for these animals are deprived of sacrificial essence (are impure)." Commenting upon this passage, Prof: Max Muller remarks: [1] "The drift of this story is most likely that in former times all these victims had been offered. We know it for certain that in case of horses and oxen, though afterwards these sacrifices were discontinued. As to sheep and goats, they were considered proper victims to a later time. When vegetable offerings took the place of bloody victims, it was clearly the

1. *History of Ancient Sanskrit Literature.* p. 420.

wish of the author of our passage to show that, for certain sacrifices these rice-cakes were as efficient as the flesh of animals:" The theory of the sacrificial cake proving as efficacious as the animal victim is well advanced in *Satapatha Brahmana*. I. 2, 3, 5. according to which the sacrificial cake to be offered at the altar transforms itself into an animal victim; rather, to put it correctly, an animal victim is invoked into the substance of the cake and then it is offered. "As it is an animal sacrifice that this sacrificial cake is offered." Dr. Julius Eggeling in a foot-note to this verse says that "the sacrificial cake is a substitute or symbol (*pratima*) for the animal sacrifice (as this it would be seen was originally a substitute for the human sacrifice) by which the sacrificer redeems himself from the gods." [1] Henceforwards, the sacrificial food has come to consist of butter and the butter oblation seems to have become the vogue at sacrifices throughout the succeeding ages. Characteristically enough, the butter oblation itself became hallowed and *Satapatha Brahmana* concludes: [2] "The sacrificial food at these offerings consists of clarified butter. Now the butter, indeed, is a thunderbolt, and with thunderbolt, the butter, the gods gained the seasons, the years and deprived their rivals of the

1. *Satapatha Brahmana XI. I, 8, 3,* and *Taittareya Brahmana III.* 2, 8, 8. It is interesting to note here that there is a certain amount of historicity given to this idea by the fact that later kings like Gopaditya and Meghavahana, especially the latter, who, while abstaining from slaughter of animals are reported to have specially substituted the effigy of an animal in ghee in preference to a regular animal victim originally offered at sacrifices. Cf. *Rajatarangini*. I. 344 and III. 7. Stein, Vol. I. pp. 51 and 72 respectively.

2. *Satapatha Brahmana.* I. 5. 3, 4,

seasons of the year. And with thunderbolt, the butter, he now, in the same way, gains the seasons, the year and deprives his enemies of the seasons of the year. For this reason, clarified butter forms the sacrificial food at these offerings. Now this butter is the year's own liquor: hence the gods gained it (the year) by means of of its own liquor. This is the reason why clarified butter forms the sacrificial food at these (fire-offerings)". Again,[1] the butter portions must be offered to the Prajapati. As the Prajapati is undefined, the butter libation offered also becomes undefined, exalted, and "verily by means of the sacrifice the gods made that conquest of the heavens." All the while we have to remember that in the accounts of the relations between gods and men we have to imagine a constant fight between the gods and the *asuras*, or symbolically, between good and evil, light and darkness, to attain the former of which the human being on earth must perform sacrifices through the efficacy of which alone he will attain his ends.

We will now take up the several theories that hallow the name of the cow with a sacredness of its own,—theories developed with a deliberate will on the part of the orthodox Hindu, mostly with a his orical and observant basis, that made the cow appear as the divine embodiment of plenty and prosperity.

Dr. Macdonnel writes: [2] "Among the domestic animals known to Rig *Veda*......cattle, however, occupy the chief place. Cows were the chief form of wealth and the name of sacrificial 'fee', *dakshina*, is properly

1. *Satapatha Brahmana.* I. 6, 1. 20-21 and I. 6, 2, 1.
2. *A History of Sanskrit Literature*, p. 149.

an adjective meaning 'right', 'valuable', with the ellipse of *go*, 'cow'. No sight gladdens the eye of the Vedic Indians more than the cow returning from the pasture and licking her calf fastened by a cord; no sound was more musical to his ear than the lowing of the milch kine. To him, therefore, there was nothing grotesque in the poet exclaiming, "as the cows low to their calves near the stalls, so we praise Indra with our hymns" or 'like unmilked kine we have called aloud (lowed) to thee, O! hero (Indra)'". This is the superb attitude of the Aryans which made them weave a web of praise and glory round the name of the cow and thus lend her a grand appearance. In this they were totally unblinded by their enthusiasm, as it always appealed to experience and hard actualities of agricultural life which demand a meticulous conserving of bovine life.

Dr. Jacobi opines in his invaluable article on the 'cow' in the *Encyclopaedia of Religion and Ethics*[1] that the belief in the sanctity of the cow which is a prominent feature of Hinduism is traceable to pre-historic times before the Aryans separated from the Indo-Iranians. His contention is true in a great measure as we find not a less-striking similarity between the ideas of the *Zend-Avesta* and the Aryan sacred lore, which we shall see later on in the chapter on the Zoroastrian attitude.[2] In the *Zend-Avesta* we meet with a divine being called *Geus-Urvan* (*Goshurun*), the soul of the cow which is identified with the personification and guardian of living beings,

1. Vol. IV. p. 224–226.

2. Dr. Jacobi's article is of immense usefulness to the student of ancient Hindu literature, especially in getting a clear idea of the influence wielded by the cow upon Aryan thought and wisdom. Almost all the available data have been brought to bear upon his observations.

whereas in the *Adharva Veda* Vasa,[1] the prototype of cows, is a kind of the generating principle of the universe.[2]

In the Vedic times the word *go* used to suggest among other things the following meanings and was almost used as a synonym for them : earth, heaven, rays of light, speech and singer.[3] More especially the cow is identified with the earth. In the *Adharva Veda*,[4] Viraj, the divine cow, is described as having come down upon earth: "She ascended; she came to men; men called to her : 'O rich in cheer, come!'; of her, Manu, son of Vaivasvant, was young ;[5] earth was vessel ; her, Prithi, son of Vena milked ; from her he milked both cultivation and grain."[6] In this hymn is contained the myth so elaborately worked out in *Vishnu Purana*[7] which runs as follows : "Prithu son of Vena having been constituted universal monarch desired to recover from his subjects edible plants, which, during the preceding period of anarchy, had all perished. He therefore assailed the earth, which, assuming the form of a cow, fled from him and traversed all the heavenly regions. At last she yielded to him, and promised to fecundate the soil with her milk. Thereupon, Prithu flattened the surface of the earth with his bow, uprooting and thrusting away hundreds and thousands of mountains. Having made

1. X. 10.
2. In this connection see Sir Monier-Williams : *Brahmanism and Hinduism.* p. 319.
3. See Jacobi. *Op. Cit.*
4. VIII. 22—29.
5. Literally, 'calf'.
6. *Harvard Oriental Series. VIII.* 514.
7. I. xiii. Wilson's Translation.

Swayambhuva Manu the calf, he milked the Earth and received the milk into his own hands for the benefit of mankind. Thence proceeded all kinds of corn and vegetable upon which people subsist now and always. By granting life to the Earth, Prithu was as her father; and she thence derived the patronymic appellation *prthivi* (daughter of Prithu). Then the gods, the sages, the demons, the Gandharvas, Yaksas, Pitrs, Serpents, Mountains, and trees took a milking vessel suited to their kind, and milked the Earth of appropriate milk. And the milker and the calf were both peculiar to their own species".

This is the reason why the cow is regarded in India as a *mata*, a mother, and thus the *gomata* receives the unremitting love and sincere veneration of the generality of the Hindu population. As Dr. Jolly puts it,[1] "the mythical identification of the earth with a cow furnishes the basis of many poetical conceits, eg., that a king should milk the earth tenderly in order to get plentiful revenue etc." She is the most auspicious creature on earth besides being purity and plenty incarnate. Thus "cows are auspicious purifiers and upon the cows depend the world."[2] "A house is purified by scouring it with a broom and plastering it with cow-dung, and a manuscript or a book by sprinkling water over it. Land is cleansed by scouring, by plastering it with cow-dung, by sprinkling, by scraping, by

1. *Encyclopaedia of Religion and Ethics*. Vol. IV. *Art.* Cow (Hindu)

2. *Institutes af Vishnu.* XXIII. 57. Trans. Julius Jolly. S. B. E., Vol. VII. p. 105.

burning, or by letting cows (or goats) pass (a day and night) on it."[1] This is in extreme harmony with hygienic principles as, cow-dung, as we shall see subsequently in the chapter on the medicinal values of the products of the cow, is at once antiseptic and a bactericide. The religious sanctity of the cow added a further degree of sacerdotal importance to cow-dung as a purificatory agent. This superb attitude of veneration of the cow and the deeming sacrosanct of the faintest expression of the values of mother cow culminates in that verse of *Vishnusutra* which sings:[2] "In the urine of the cows dwells the Ganges, prosperity (dwells) in the dust (rising from their couch), good-fortune in cow-dung, and virtue in saluting them. Therefore, they should be constantly saluted." Place side by side with this another verse of the Vedic hymnal[3] which muses, "like the bright heated butter of the cow (the appearance) of the god is lovely, like the bountifulness of the milch cow," and the Hindu attitude towards the cow explains itself with remarkable amplitude. It is interesting to note the story related in the *Mahabharata*[4] about the sanctity of the urine of cows. "Sri, the goddess of fortune, who left the demons for the gods, came to the cows, desiring to reside in them. They would, however, have nothing to do with that fickle deity, but in the end they were moved by her entreaties and consented to honour her. Do thou live in our

1 *Institutes of Vishnu.* Ch. XXIII. vs. 56-57.

2 *Ibid.* v. 61.

3 *Vedic Hymns*: Part II. IV. 1.6. Translated by Hermann Oldenberg. S.B.E. Vol. XLVI. p. 308.

4 *Mahabharata.* XIII. 82.

urine and dung; both these are sacred, O! auspicious goddess.'"

Cows are the daughters of heavenly Surabhi, which means literally the fragrant one. from the peculiar smell of the cow, and created by *Prajapati* from his breath. The story of the birth of this heavenly Surabhi is admirably told in the greatest Epic of India. [1] According to this myth, "Daksha, the creater, for the sake of beings he had created drank a quantity of nectar. He became gratified with the nectar he had quaffed, and thereupon an erectation came out, diffusing an excellent perfume all round. As the result of that erectation, Daksha saw that it gave birth to a cow which he called Surabhi. This Surabhi was thus a daughter of his, which had sprung from his mouth. The cow called Surabhi brought forth a number of cows, which came to be regarded as the mothers of the world." Side by side with this may be put the idea of *Kamadhenu* or celestial cow akin to those of *Goshurun*, the soul of the cow as we meet in the *Zend-Avesta*, already referred to above, and *Pouru Samedha Gaus* the couple born of the only created bull out of which sprang up two-hundred and eighty species, as we shall see in the chapter on the Zoroastrian attitude. *Kamadhenu* along with its associate abstraction of plenty—the *Kalpa Vrikhsha*, meets the needs of all classes of votaries without distinction of comparative accessibility of the articles cherished. The Bull of Sankara, as we have to take the idea of the sacerdotal and symbolical importance of bovine cattle, is typical of *matter* belonging to the mundane world, and its conspicuous position in the Hindu temples represents the

1. *Ibid.* XIII. 77.

relationship between *pasu* (matter) and *pathi* (spirit) as they are techincally called in Saiva philosophy. In the *Ramayana* is that familiar story of the cow of plenty in possession of sage Jamadagni which was attempted to be stolen by Kartaviryarjuna, how Rama son of Jamadagni killed the latter and restored it to its lawful owner, how the sons of Karthavirya slew Jamadagni in the absence of Rama, and how Rama finally avenged the death of that pious sage. The passage in the *Ramayana* which describes the qualities of that wonderful cow of plenty helps us in a great measure to understand the mythical and symbolical qualities of the cow of plenty that came into existence when the sea of milk was churned by the Devas and Rakshasas with Mandara mountain as the churn and Vasuki serpent as the line in their quest after *amrita*, the celestial nectar and elixir of life. According to this passage of the *Ramayana*: [1]

> "The cow from whom all plenty flows
> Obedient to their saintly lord,
> Viands to suit each taste outpoured.
> Honey she gave, and roasted grain
> Mead with sweet flowers, and sugarcane.
> Each beverage of flavour rare.
> And food of every sort were there:
> Hills of hot rice, and sweetened cakes,
> And curdled milk, and soup in lakes,
> Vast breakers flowing to the brim
> With sugared milk prepared for him;
> Aud dainty sweet-meats deftly made
> Before the hermit's guests were laid."

Such, in short, are the potentialities of *Kamadhenu*, the celestial cow.

1. In this connection see *Hindu Theology, Vedic and Puranic.* pp. 167-168. by Mr. W. J. Williams. (1900) Thacker Spink. Calcutta.

There is a cow-heaven or *Go-Loka* which we often meet with in the Epics and Puranas.[1] It is the abode of heavenly Surabhi. According to the popular theory, the *Goloka* is above the three worlds, which is delineated as a paradise, the most beautiful place to live in, which was brought into being and assigned to the mother of the cows by Brahma who was quite pleased with the austerities of the former. According to another tradition,[1] Surabhi has her abode in *Rasatala* the last but one of the underworlds with her four daughters the *dikpalis*. Residence in the *Go-Loka* is the choicest cherishing of a departing soul, and it is only attainable through piety and austerity, one of the efficacious means of attaining the end being the vindication of human *largesse* in the shape of the free distribution of cows according to set customs and formalities among deserving people.

Note must here be taken of the super-importance which cows attained due to the association of Sre Krishna, the incarnation of Vishnu, with herdsmen and cows during the course of his earthly ministry. Krishna spent his childhood among cows and *gopis*, the daughters of herdsmen. Lord Krishna, that age famous paragon of cadences, lured both the cow and the *gopi* with the melodious chant of his flute. It is but a familiar sight to the average Hindu to imagine Lord Krishna rallying round him all the citizens of Brindavan as well as all the cows in the neighbourhood under the shade of Mandaragiri mountain which he held up with his own hand to

1. In this connection see Jacobi. Op. *Cit*,
2. *Mahabharata*. XII. 102.

afford cover to man and beast on that day of dreadful avalanche. Dr. Jacobi remarks in this connection[1] that "this fact illustrates the high reputation which resulted from the connection with cows, since herdsmen were thought the first guardians and companions of the highest god."

Alongside of this, the consecration of the bulls and letting them loose as privileged beings to roam at their will and draw respect from all people is to be noted with particular interest. It is a familiar fact that the bull is sacred to Siva, the god of destruction (*laya*), in the Hindu Trinity. Consecrating bulls and letting them loose is an age-long practice, and is in all probability a relic of the queer old Vedic practice of sacrificing cows and other animals on the death of a human being, already noticed above. This old practice has undergone a transformation with the changed attitude of the Aryans towards the cow, and on the occasion of the death of a male member of a family, his relations consecrate a bull of distinctive features according to *sastraic* rules and ritual and let it loose to wander at liberty. The freedom and privileges of the Brahmani bull are inviolate and even destructive work done by the bull cannot, under ordinary circumstances, be taken into account. This is one of the features of the Hindu provisions towards the propagation and preservation of the bovine species in India. Sir Monier-Williams sees in it, and that rightly too, the "happy forethought" of the Hindus "but for which this useful animal might have been exterminated in time of famine." The Brahmani

1. *Loc. Cit,*

bull supplies the necessary cover to the Indian cow, and in the absence of any scientific method of breeding cattle, it supplies a potential agency for producing the best strains of Indian cattle. That the idea of consecration of bulls is quite an early one cannot be disputed. The latest excavations of the Archaeological Department at Mahanjo Daro and Harappa in the Punjab prove this point beyond doubt. In the course of an article to *The Times*, London, on *Prehistoric India*, Sir John Marshall, Director General of Archaeology with the Government of India observes: "Of those recovered by Mr. Dikshit last season, the most striking, perhaps, is one depicting a Brahmani bull, the drawing of which shows great breadth and a fine sense of the decorative. Incidentally, it may be remarked, *this seal also proves that the breed of the Brahmani bulls was every whit as good* 5,000 *years ago as it is to-day*." [1]

Dr. Jacobi speaks of the practical effect of the veneration of the cow on the Hindu religion. [2] A profound sense of veneration and attachment invested the name of the cow with a sacerdotal halo of super-importance that every act concerning the treatment of the cow and her products should be done with strict vigilance according to the inculcations of the *sastras*. "The cow became the centre of a peculiar worship, with proper *mantras* [3] and rites. The devotees have to recite the names of cows, and to bow their heads in reverence to them, [4] and they were enjoined to subsist on the five

1. The *italics* are mine.
2. *Encyclopaedia of Religion and Ethics*. Art. Cow (Hindu).
3. *Mahabharata*. XIII. 80. 1-3; 78. 246.
4. *Ibid*, 78. 16.

products of the cow, to bathe using cow-dung at the time etc. For some religious purposes, the devotees had to live and to sleep among cows in a cow-pen, or to follow a cow everywhere, as did Dilipa in the story told in the second book of Raghuvamsa." [1]

I will now conclude this chapter with a significant passage from the pen of Sir Monier-Williams which strikingly summarises within the compass of a few sentences the superb attitude of the Hindus towards the cow. [2] " In the forefront must be placed the worship of the cow and the bull. The utility of the cow as a source of nourishment to a people who never kill animals for food and of the ox and bull to the agriculturists who have no cart-horses for draught, is manifest. The cow is of all animals the most sacred. Every part of its body is inhabited by some deity or other. Every hair on its body is inviolable. All its excreta are hallowed. Not a particle ought to be thrown away as impure. On the contrary, the water it ejects ought to be preserved as the best of holy waters—*a semi-destroying liquid*—which sanctified everything it touched, while nothing purifies like the cow-dung. Any spot which a cow has condescended to honour with the sacred deposit of her excrement is for ever afterwards consecrated ground, and the filthiest place plastered with it is at once cleansed and freed from pollution, [3] while the ashes produced

1. Jacobi. *Loc. Cit.*

2. Sir Monier-Williams. *Brahmanism and Hinduism*, pp. 317-19. London. John Murray. (Fourth Edn.) 1891.

3. Sir Monier-Williams' description of the popular belief among the Hindus about the efficacy of cow-dung and urine as purificatory agents has a symbolical and physical sense. We have so far seen the symbolical or religious side of it. The physical side will be seen in the chapter on the medicinal values of the products of the cow under the therapeutic value of urea.

by burning this hallowed substance are of such a holy nature that they not only make clean all material things, however previously unclean, but have only to be sprinkled over a sinner to convert him into a saint. . . . . . . As to the bull, he is dedicated to Siva, and constantly associated with the god as typical of generative power. Images of him are to be found in all Linga temples. The letting lose of a bull (*vrishotsarga* or *brishotsarga*)—stamped with Siva's pendant —in cities like Benares and Gaya is fraught with the highest merit."

CHAPTER IV.

THE TEACHINGS OF BUDDHA.

THE religion, or more correctly, the order of life that emphasises with the Jain creed the supreme dictum of life—*ahimsa paramo dharma*, Buddhism stands out as one of the prominent bulwarks against any infringement of life on earth, and preaches the most humane attitude towards the sanctity of life, human as well as animal. The Bodhisatta lived an exemplary life and preached it to the world. The *Lakkhana Suttanta* thus emphasises this phase of the *Buddha's* life : [1]

> " No living thing he harmed, by hand, by scourge,
> By clod, by sword, by any murderous death,
> By bonds or threats, no injury he wrought.
> Therefore in blissful borne, he reaped the fruit
> Of happiness, found happy things for deeds."

Asoka, the supreme apologist and apostle of Buddhism, gave a regal colouring to this humane attitude to life and actually strove his best to bring about an era of peace and amity between the human and the animal worlds. His Rock Edict I. and Pillar Edict V. in particular, and his theory of *dharma* in general, stand out as testimonies to this statement. [2] The Buddhist monk perpetuates this creed even at the present day where-

1. *Dialogues of the Buddha*. Part III. Translated by Mr. and Mrs. Rhys Davids. Sacred Books of the Buddhists series. Vol. IV. p. 157. (1921).

2. See Dr. D. R. Bhandarkar. Carmichael Lectures on *Asoka*. 1923. Calcutta University Press. 1925. pp. 273 and 314-15 respectively. The edicts are quoted in full in the chapter on the History of Cow Protection in India.

ever Buddhism holds even the slightest sway. One of the supreme qualifications of a person belonging to the Buddhist *sangha* or Order, in order to attain *arhantship*, is to practice the ways of humaneness and to live the life of exemplary humaneness.

This is, in short, the general legacy of Buddhism to the world. In this respect Buddhism owes a deep debt to the creed of Mahavira that saw its inception a few decades earlier. Jainism can never be beaten by any other ethical creed in the world in respect of this supreme selfless endeavour of man to respect animal life. The daily life of an average Jain is an excellent lesson in showing forth the sacred character of life on earth, human as well as animal. This prominent characteristic of the Jaina creed as propounded by Mahavira twenty-five centuries ago has remained intact even at the present day. To feel compassion for the sufferings of a live being is one of the instincts of man, as will be seen more fully when we treat of the humanitarian view-point. This is a perennial stream of sympathy which sees no end, nor feels the force of any intermediary impediment. The Jains perpetuate this special feature of their creed to the end of the world. To Jainism need not be applied the test of the numerical strength of its followers, as the popular mind would do, to ascertain its genuineness. The excellence of the ethical code and the exemplary ideal set before the world are to be the criteria from which a religion ought to be judged. This touch-stone of merit shows to the world that Jainism need not in any way fear about the stability of her position among religions in respect of this profoundly humane religious code of the sanctity of life. A glance at the Jaina hospital at Allahabad will prove this beyond doubt.[1] A retrospective survey of the history of Akbar and the influence of the Jaina *acharyas* over his ecclectic spirit that made him grant a *firman* prohibiting animal slaughter in his dominions, as preserved in the Sanscrit inscription on the porch of the Adiswara temple, in the Satrunjaya hills, near Palitana in Rajaputana, shows to the world the moral exertion of the Jains to make proselytes to their creed from other religions and see to the spread of their teachings.[2]

With this legacy as it basis, Buddhism evolved her own distinct moral code. Besides pleading for the abolition of caste distinctions and equalising the *snatakas* when once they embrace the rules of the *sangha* Buddhism did away openly with all forms of ritual. Ritual formed the back-bone of Brahmanical superiority and supremacy. Sacrifice is the central hinge upon which the Brahmanical ministry of the world moved. This phase of Brahmanical superiority is admirably summed up by Dr. Shamasastri in his *Evoution of Indian Polity*:[3] "It was his sacrifice that averted draught by causing timely rains. It was his sacrifice that ensured timely victory to the king over his enemy. It was his

1. See the article by L. Morseby on "Man and Beast in India" in *The Herald of The Golden Age.* Quoted in *The Jaina Gazette.* Vol. XXI. No 7. July. 1925. pp. 207-13. (Madras).

2. See the introduction by S. N. Banerjee to *The Commentary of Father Monserrate.* Humphry Milford. 1922. p. v. Cf. *Bhandarkar Commemoration Volume.* Article on "The Jain Teachers of Akbar." by V. A. Smith. pp. 265-276. Bhandarkar Oriental Institute. Poona. 1917.

3. P. 89. Calcutta University Press. 1920.

sacrifice that brought in a plentiful harvest. It was his sacrifice and medical amulet that introduced concord between the king and the people. In short there was no public or private activity that is not attended with a sacrificial performance. His memory was so strong that he remembered a number of suitable prayers which he alone knew to interpret. He alone knew to perform sacrifices so correctly as to ensure success. His failure to achieve expected success was due to insufficiency of sacrifices. Thus he was a God incarnate to the people of the times." Sacrifice would mean sacrifice of animal victims. The wide range of animal victims capable of being butchered is marked in Brahmanical ritual. [1] Even live-stock, bulls and cows, which are essential for the economic progress of society were at one time offered at sacrifices in ancient Aryavarta, as we have already seen in the previous chapters. [2] This is the crucial point which the *Buddha* caught hold of for reproof. To him external and outward show of faith is odious. His respect towards animal life was exemplary. Hence Buddha made it his stock missile in discomfiting his Brahman adversaries during his own life-time. This is what we learn from the Jatakas. This is the sum total of the Buddhist tradition of the Mahayana type. [3]

As expressed by Dr. Berridale Keith: [4] "The morality of action predominates in the Buddhist view, and

---

1. Cf. *Satapatha Brahmana.* I 2. 3. 6-7.

2. "It is declared in the *Vagasaneyaka* that milch-cows and oxen are fit for sacrifices." *Vasistha Dharmasastra.* xiv. 44-46. Translated by F. Max Muller. S.B.E. Vol. XIV. p. 74. Cf. *A History of Sanscrit Literature.* By Dr. A. A. Macdonnel. p. 125. (1905.)

3. Cf. *Kutadanta Sutta. Dialogues of the Buddha.* Part I. Translated by T. W. Rhys Davids. S.B.B. Vol. II. p. 174 ff.

4. *Buddhist Philosophy in India and Ceylon.* p. 114. By. Dr. A. Berridale Keith. D.C.L., D. Litt., Oxford. 1923.

ritualistic practices such as sacrifice and purification, nay even offerings to the dead, become merely surplusage, superstitious usages (*silabbata*) which have no value." Again, take another passage from the pen of Dr. Rhys Davids :[1] "That a sacrifice of the heart is better than a sacrifice of bullocks, the ethical more worthy than any physical sacrifice is simply the more sensible, rational and more human view of the matter." These two passages put in a nut-shell the attitude of Buddhism towards sacrifice. Several stories are preserved in the Jatakas about the abhorrence of the Buddhist towards the Brahmanical type of sacrifice, as we understand best from the description of Dr. Sylvain Levi, the acknowledged àuthority on the subject. The learned French Savant says:[2] "It is difficult to imagine anything more brutal and more material than the theology of the Brahmanas. Notions which usage afterwards gradually refined, and clothed with a garb of morality, take us aback by their savage realism...... Morality finds no place in this system. Sacrifice which regulates the relation of man to the divinities, is a mechanical act, operating by its own spontaneous energy (*par son energie intime*) ; and that, hidden in the bosom of nature, is only brought out by the magic of the priest." This is the relationship that exists between the Brahmanical and Buddhist theories of sacrifice. The marked contrast of these theories to each other is obvious, while the superiority of the Buddhist attitude is easily discernible. In the light of this relationship we will now set

1. *Dialogues of the Buddha.* Part I. S. B. B. Vol. II. p. 164.

2. *Doctrine Du Sacrifice Ches Lez Brahmanas*: p. 9. (Paris. 198). Quoted in Rhys Davids, *Buddhist India.* pp. 240-241. London. T. Fisher Unwin. 1903.

ourselves to examine the Buddhist sacred texts as far as they throw light on the Buddhist attitude towards sacrifice, and its attitude towards animal life as far as it touches kine-life even though it be in a faint degree.

Mrs. Rhys Davids writes in the *Encyclopaedia of Religion and Ethics*:[1] "The attitude of Buddhism towards every kind of external sacrifice was one of uncompromising dissent. It judged such ritual to be the futile expression of misdirected outlay and effort, and in some of its forms involves cruelty. And the kind of benefits hoped for from the rites was not sufficiently, as we should say, spiritual." This excerpt is amply borne out by the contents of the Jaṭakas and Suttas as they come down to us. Brahmans and recluses who perform sacrifices to Agni belong to that class of people who live by low arts and "Gotama the recluse holds aloof from those low arts."[2] The life of a Bhikku must be an exemplary life of mercifulnesss, and he must abstain from killing any living being, and strip off all roughness.[3] According to *Samyukta*. 176 :

> "Where divers goats and sheep and kine are slain,
> Never to such a rite as that repair
> The noble seers who walk the perfect way."

Slaughter of life was reprehensible in the "great sacrifice." Bodhisatta trumpets a loud admonition to the Brahmans and eloquently harps upon the cruelty involved in sacrifice.[4]

---

1. Vol. XI. p. 7. (1920).
2. *Brahmajala Sutta*; i. 21. *Dialogues of the Buddha.* part I. S. B. B. Vol. II. pp. 17-19. (1923.)
3. *Samanna Phala Sutta.* 43. *Ibid.* p. 79.
4. *Jataka.* Vol. VI. No. 543.

"If he who kills is counted innocent,

Let Brahmins Brahmins kill......
We see no cattle asking to be slain
That they a new and better life may gain.
Rather they go unwilling to their death,
And in vain struggles yield their last breath.
To veil the post, the victim and the blow,
The Brahmins let their choicest rhetoric flow.
....
These cruel cheats, as ignorant as vile,
Weave their long frauds the innocent to beguile."

Further, sacrificial rites were intended to further low aspirations. "The transformation and spiritualisation of the two aspects of sacrifice—as symbol and as self-devotion—are emphasised by Buddhism as they were by Hebrew Psalmist and Prophet."[1] According to *Samyukta*. i. 169. sacrificial celebrations of the Buddhist type are no more matters for surplusage and external manifestation, but the inwardness of the motives of the person sacrificing is identified with the personal immolation of self, which means attainment of *nirvana*. Thus the Buddhist taunts his Brahman contemporary, according to this *Sutta*:

"I lay no wood, Brahmin, for fires on altars.
Only within, beneath the fire I kindle.
Even my fire burns; ever tense and ardent,
I, Arhant, work out the life that is holy.
....the heart's the altar,
The fire thereon, this is man's self well tamed."

1. In this respect see the *Encyclopaedia of Religion and Ethics*. Vol. XI. Article on Sacrifice (*Buddhist*), by C. A. F. Rhys Davids, M. A..

The Buddhist type of sacrifice is a personal one, the fires of which are inextinguishable, but last for ever.

I have got to take notice of two anecdotes in greater detail, where in the Buddha is represented to have taken an active part in completly vanquishing his Brahmanical antagonists by means of arguments and personal example. The first is *Kutadanta Sutta* to which Dr. Rhys Davids attaches much importance [1] in having won the battle over the Brahmanical theories "by the combined ridicule and earnestness of our Sutta [which] will have had its share in bringing about the victory." According to this Sutta, [2] Kutadanta was a Brahman potentate, enjoying a fief from Bimbisara. A huge sacrifice was being ordered by Kutadanta, " and a hundred bulls, and a hundred steers, and a hundred rams, had been brought to the post for sacrifice." Gotama Buddha happened to visit Khanumata, the seat of Kutadanta, during one of his mendicant travels. The proud Brahman heard about Gotama who alone "understands about the successful performance of a sacrifice with its three-fold method and its sixteen accessory instruments." He, along with other Brahmans, called upon Gotama to hear him expound his method of sacrifice. Gotama received him in a befitting manner and related the sacrifice performed by Maha Vijita (Wide-Realm), the most accomplished and virtuous man on earth, which partook of no bloody offering to the deity ; but " with ghee and oil, and butter and milk

1. *Dialogues of the Buddha.* Part I. S. B. B. Vol. II. p. 165. Cf. *The Social Organisation of North-East India in Buddha's Time.* p. 226. By Dr. Richard Fick. Translated by Dr. S. K. Maitra. Calcutta University Press. 1920.

2. S. B, B. Vol. II. pp, 173-185.

and honey and sugar only was the sacrifice accomplished." The Brahmans, including Kutadanta, were fully impressed with this mode of sacrifice and craved of Gotama to instruct them whether there are any higher kinds of sacrifice. Gotama, to their satisfaction, ends with a passage from the *Samanna Phala Sutta*. Ultimately, Kutadanta embraces the Order and begins his life straight away as a Bhikku.

The second one is the *Story of the Sacrifice* as it is preserved in the *Jatakamala.*[1] According to this story, Bodhisatta was a prince royal having obtained his kingdom by hereditary descent. With characteristic relevance suited to the times, the *purohita* approaches him to advice the performance of a sacrifice to bring about ample rainfall.[2] Gotama puts two relevant queries which utterly baffle the Brahmans and render them tongue-tied. They are worthy of remembrance. "And should the victim killed in sacrifice really go to heaven, should we not expect the Brahmanas to offer themselves to be immolated in sacrifice? A similar practice, however, is nowhere seen among them. Who, then, may take to heart the advice proferred by these counsellors?

"As to the Celestials, should we believe that they who are wont to enjoy the fair ambrosia of incomparable scent, flavour, magnificence and effective power, served

---

1. *The Jatakamala.* x. "The Story of the Sacrifice." Translated by J. S. Speyer. S. B. B. Vol. I. pp. 94-96. London. Henry Froude. Oxford University Press. 1895.

2. On the influence of the *Purohita* upon the kings of the Buddhist times, see, Fick, *Social Organisation*, pp. 175, 222 and 224-26. Cf. the Hindu Kings and the influence wielded upon them by the *purohitas* in Shamasastri, *Evolution of Indian Polity*. Lect. V. "The Duties and Prerogatives of Kings and Priests." pp. 88-98. Calcutta University Press. 1920.

to them by the beautiful Apsarasas as would abandon it to delight in the slaughter of a victim, that they might feast on the amentum and such other parts of his body as are offered to them in sacrifice?" To fully drive home the import of his teachings, Gotama ordered a *purushamedha*, or human sacrifice of all the wicked persons in his realm. This stratagem had the desired effect and wickedness was totally stamped out, as the story goes on. Gotama then distributes wealth among his subjects and he is praised by one and all for his wisdom and *largesse*.

The teachings of Buddhism were largely instrumental in stamping out the excessive resort taken to sacrifice in Brahmanical India. Dr. Fick sums up this effect in the following manner: [1] "The conclusion of this Jataka [2] as well as similar narratives—for instance, the story of the prince who terminates a sacrifical ceremony in his kingdom by a tournament and further the prohibition of the slaughter of animals in the Ayakuta Jataka (III. 146)—point to this, that with the spread of Buddhist doctrines the cult of sacrifice gradually declined." Even as late as the fifth century of the Christian era, Kalhana mentions in his *Rajatarangini* that Meghavahana, one of the kings of Kashmir, on account of his respect for animal life, used the effigy of an animal made with ghee for a sacrifice. [3] The effect of Buddhism upon the Brahmanical theory of sacrifice is

1 *Sacial Organisation*, p. 226.

2 *Lohakhumbha Jataka*.

3 *Rajatarangini*, iii. 7. Translated by Dr. M. Aurel Stein, M.A., Ph. D., Westminster. Archibald Constable. 2 Vols. 1900. Vol. I. p. 72.

so decided, that at the present day we find sacrifices of the early Brahmanical type rarely taking place in India.

One more point remains to be examined. It is the Buddhist attitude to wealth and towards cattle in particular. Asoka best sums up the Buddhist attitude to wealth in one of his Rock Edicts wherein he says, "meritorious is small expense and small accumulation." [1] This is Buddhism's legacy to its followers, the Bhikkus. In the *Chakkavatti Silnada Suttanta* is another passage which is more explicit than Asoka's in preaching love, charity, abstinence and poverty [2] "And what is the meaning of the wealth for a brother? Herein that a brother abides, letting his mind fraught with love, pervade one quarter of the world, and so too the second quarter, and so the third and so the fourth. And thus, the whole wide world, above, below, around, and everywhere and altogether does he continue to pervade with love-burdened thought, abounding sun-shine and beyond measure, free from hatred and ill-will."

With all this detachment of the Buddhists towards wealth, their veneration of animal life is pronounced and exemplary. Their love of cattle is explicit. The Buddhists recognise them as a fundamental economic factor indispensable to social progress, the *sangha* being essentially a democratic body. They enjoin upon the king the duty of specially protecting the people who are engaged in cattle-breeding and agriculture. Thus

1 *Rock Edict III*. Bhandarkar. *Asoka*. p. 278.

2 *Dialogues of the Buddha.* Part III. S.B.B. Vol. IV. p. 76. Translated by Mr. and Mrs. Rhys Davids, 1921.

says the *Kutadanta Sutta*: [1] "Whosoever there be in the king's realm, who devote themselves to keeping cattle and the farm, to them let the king give food and corn." Kautilya describing the system of polity and economics prevalent in the days of the flourish of Buddhism emphasises the superiority of grazing cattle and developing pastures over agriculture. [2] The cow always appealed most to the Buddhists. There were special superintendents appointed over cows in the early Buddhist times. [3] The appearance of a cow is a superlative quality of beauty and exaltedness. [4] With its supreme veneration of animal life, its abhorrence of sacrifice, its exalted attitude to cow's life, Buddhism ranks among the major religions of the world in conserving cow life.

As a prominent feature of the Buddhist attitude, the institution of the *pinjrapole* or animal hospital may be sketched here, even though fuller details will be given later on. From time immemorial animal hospitals were flourishing in India. An encouragement to the establishment of such charitable institutions was given in the time of the Buddhist rulers of India. Animal sacrifice was prohibited, as a knowledge of anatomy is essential in victimising the consecrated brute. Asoka prohibits even the castration of bulls in his Pillar Edict V. as it

1. Verse 11. *Dialogues of the Buddha* Part I. S.B.B. Vol. II. p. 176. (1923).

2. *Arthasastra* Book VIII. Ch. iv. Translated by Dr. R. Shamasastri. 2nd. Edn. 1923. p. 389.

3. *Ibid.* Book V. Chapter xxix. *Ibid.* pp. 155-159.

4. *Dialogues of the Buddha.* Part III. *Lakkhana Suttanta.* 10. Translated by Mr. and Mrs. Rhys Davids. S.B.B. Vol. IV. p. 157, (1921).

involves cruelty.[1] Buddha is reputed to have established animal hospitals besides preventing animal sacrifices, and in his time ancient Indian medicine received the greatest stimulus even though surgery was allowed to languish.[2] Asoka is reputed to have appointed *dharma*-officers who preached the doctrine of *anarambho prananam* and *avihisa bhutanam.* In his Rock Edict II. Asoka mentions that he "established medical treatment of two kinds—that wholesome for men, and that wholesome for animals."[3] Commenting upon this, Dr. Bhandarkar adduces a wealth of evidenee towards the fact that *pinjrapoles*, the establisment of which to protect crippled and aged cows is pressed very much at the present-day in India, owe their origin to the exertions of Asoka, and were carefully preserved at least in the Bombay presidency under the protection of the Mahratta chiefs of the XVII and the XVIII centuries[4].

1 Bhandarkar. *Asoka* p. 315.

2 *A Short History of Aryan Medical Science* p. 189. by H. H. Sir Bhagvat Sinh Jee. The Thakore Saheb or Gondol. M.D., D.C.L., LL.D., F.R.S.E.. London, Macmillan and Co., 1896.

3 Bhandarkar. *Asoka.* p. 276.

4. *Ibid.* pp. 184-85.

CHAPTER V.

ZARATHUSTRA AND HIS RELIGION.

OF all the religions that rose and fell in world history, Zoroastrianism offers us, perhaps, the nearest approach to the Hindu religion and at times even outshines it, as regards the meticulous conserving of the lives of the bovine species. Like all older religions and civilizations, Zoroastrianism markedly brings religious influences to bear upon the attitude of individual human beings towards the highest economic interests of society. Cattle which occupy a prominent place in the material wealth of ancient civilizations engage in no mean degree the attention of the worshippers of Ahura Mazda and the followers of Zarathustra.

Zarathustra claims the Aryan heritage, since the relationship between the Aryan and the Indo-Iranian stocks is quite marked and important. This traditional and potent attachment of the Indo-Iranians to their Aryan brethren after the latter have made a permanent abode of the Punjab, makes Zarathustra expound several principles of his religious creed in the light of Aryan sagacity and scholarship. As regards several ceremonial practices, he wholesalely draws upon the stock of Arayan ritual and passes them off as the veritable emanations of his own wisdom. The great similarity which the Pahlavi language bears to Sanscrit made his task quite easy. Etymology is not far to seek, and with a few linguistic alterations and variations of inflexions the technical words such as we meet in the Aryan sacred lore are easily absorbed by the language of the *Zend-Avesta.* [1] In this respect the language of the *Zend* bears the same similitude as the Pali language of the Buddhist sacred lore does to Sanscrit. Thus the *gos* of the *Zend* is the same as the root *go* (cow) in Sanscrit. Perhaps, *gomes* (urine) of the Pahlavi language has the same root as the Sanscrit word *gomedha.* Again the *Zend* shows such a striking similarity to the *Rig Veda* as regards the element-worship, that we are led to doubt that the former might have borrowed not an inconsiderable loan of ideas and beliefs from the perennial *srutis* of the Aryans. At least both must have had a common heritage. [2] For example, the *Mithra* of the Parsis presides over almost the same functions as those performed by his counterpart in Vedic literature. One point which must be borne in mind in this connection is that the *Avesta* in general and the ritualistic portions in particular are but the revelations of Ahura Mazda, the holiest of the holies, the Supreme God, to the queries put by Zarathustra the prophet of Zoroastrianism, and are related in the direct form of speech. Unlike the Aryan ritual, the ceremonial practices propounded in the *Zend-Avesta* are the products, so to speak, of direct revelation. In this respect the ritual of the *Avesta* commands a greater influence

1 As regards this similarity, see the admirable introduction of M. James Darmesteter to his translation of the *Zend-Avesta.* S.B.E. Vol. IV.

2. Dr. Jacobi emphasises this common heritage of the Aryans and the Indo-Iranians. See *Encyclopaedia of Religion and Ethics*, Vol, IV, pp. 224-26. Art. *Cow* (Hindu.)

upon the followers of Zarathustra than do the Brahmanical ritualistic practices upon the descendants of the Indo-Aryans, as the latter are more or less stigmatised as the compiled and carefully manufactured formalities of ritual by the scrupulosity of the Hindu priesthood.

Tradition strongly points to the fact that the original text of the *Zend-Avesta* has undergone a transformation in several ways. Firstly, the original dialect in which it was written has been almost lost and the present form of the text we possess is only a restored version of the corrupted original. During the process of ages, the primeval simplicity of the *Zend* has been lost, while certain interlocutory passages about ritualistic observances have crept into the original text, due to the efforts of the Magi of Media, the officiating priesthood of the Parsis without whose ministry the Gods could not be heard. [1] Thus Darmesteter points out the change, while speaking about the Achamenian element in the *Zend-Avesta* : [2] "There were two sorts of sacrifice, the bloody sacrifice of which a survival has lingered to this day in the Atash Zohr, and the bloodless sacrifice consisting essentially of the Haoma-offering and libations, of which there is no direct mention in the classics, but which indirect evidence obliges us to ascribe to the older religion".

We are justified in assuming the bloodless character of the Zaroastrian sacrifice as it was propounded by

1. *The Zend-Avesta*: S.B.E. Vol. IV. p. lxiii.
2. *Ibid.* p. lxii.

Zarathustra. But we find reference in the *Avesta* to the practice of huge sacrifices being offered to titular deities by certain tribes of the primeval Indo-Iranian stock. Thraetaona offers a huge sacrifice to Advi Sura partaking of a wholesale immolation of cattle life. "To her did Thraetaona, the heir of the Athwya clan offer up a sacrifice in the four-cornered Varena, with a hundred male horses, a thousand oxen, ten thousand lambs." [1] But as will be shown in greater detail a little later, the fundamental principle inculcated by Zarathustra as regards the offering of sacrifices is that the votaries should always depend upon faith and prayer and avoid any slaughter of animal victims. The *Zend-Avesta* positively deplores the bad practices of some of the tribes which "make blood flow and spill it like water." [2]

Again, commenting upon Fargard VIII. 18. which enjoins upon the followers of Zarathustra the practice of smearing the selected place for the tentative disposal of the dead with ashes or with *Nirang* (*Gomez*, urine of the ox), Darmesteter points out that the *Vendidad Sada* which is the restored form of a corrupt text of the original V*endidad* contains several glosses and interlocutory portions due to the lowering of the Zoroastrian ideal to make accommodation for changing times under the instrumentality of the officiating priesthood, the Magi. [3] Ablutions and purificatory ceremonies seem to be of a later growth but we find numerous references in

1. *Aban Yast*. 33. S.B.E., Vol. XXIII p. 61.
2. *Bahram Yast*. 54. S.B.E., Vol. XXIII. p. 245.
3. *Fargard*. VIII. 18n. S.B.E., Vol. IV. p. 97.

the *Avesta* wherein these practices are fully enjoined upon the people. [1] Whatever may have been the nature of these interpolations in the text of the *Avesta*, the ritualistic practices are still clung to by the Parsis at the present day. [2]

One prominent feature about the Zoroastrian attitude towards the sacredness of the bovine species is that it is the bull and not the cow that figures most in their ritualistic pratices. By this we are not to construe that the cow suffered the worse by the extraordinary stress laid by the worshippers of Ahura Mazda on the ritualistic importance of the bull. In the greater and lesser *Sirozahs* invocations are sung towards the appeasing of the soul of the cow. [3] Thus the Parsee votary sings : We sacrifice "to the body of the cow, to the powerful *Drvaspa*, made by Mazda and holy." [4] Again in the lesser *Sirozah* we find the same invocation but with slight modification. To achieve propitiation, "we sacrifice into the soul of the bounteous cow ; we

1. I give below some references which are concerned with the purificatory value of urine and cow-dung : *Fargards* vii. 61-65 ; viii. 18, 35-37 ; and ix. 12-36. See as well Darmesteter's remarks on the purificatory functions of *Gomez* in Zoroastrian litany and ritual, S.B.E. Vol. IV. pp. lxxv and lxxix.

2. The present writer's stay at Bombay during his University career brought him into contact with several Parsee gentlemen and it is his observation that their religious fervour is quite remarkable and that they pay particular attention to their priesthood.

3. "In the greater *Sirozah* the names of the gods invoked are introduced with the word *Yazamaide*, 'we sacrifice.' In the lesser *Sirozah* there is no introductory word, the word *Khshanaothra*, 'propitiation' being understood, as can be seen in the introductory formulas to the Yasts." Note by Darmesteter, S.B.E. Vol. XXIII. p. 1.

4. *Sirozah*. i. 14. S.B.E. Vol. XXIII. p. 9.

sacrifice unto the powerful *Drvaspa*, made by Mazda and holy."[1] The destruction of any living being is an injury to *Drvaspa*.[2] The cow straying in unknown paths, being driven away, " longs for the stables" and invokes the aid of Mithra, "the lord of wide pastures."[3] While her purificatory value in ablutions stands on a par with the Aryan beliefs about the virtues of the " bounteous" cow.

But main interest concentrates upon the indispensability of the bull in Zoroastrian ritual. The Indo-Iranian stock has much in common with the Egyptian civilization that had flourished and faded away before them. To the Egyptians, the cow and the bull were supreme objects of worship, the main reason being that to the recipient of the most ancient of civilizations the fundamental importance of live-stock, especially the plenitude of the cow and the capacity of the ox, to supply motive-force can never be minimised. To them, the cow represented Hathor at one time the most popular goddess in the country.[4] "Cambyses made himself more execrable in the eyes of the Egyptians by killing the ox Apis than all the cruelties and acts of tyranny of which he was guilty in dealing with this peaceable race."[5] In another forcible passage, Abbe

1. *Sirozah*. ii, 14. *Ibid*. p. 17.
2. *Bahram Yast*. 54. *Ibid*. p. 245.
3. *Mihir Yast*. 86-7. *Ibid*. p. 141.
4. *Studies in Indian Life and Sentiment*. By Sir Bampfylde Fuller. K.C.S.I., C.I.E., London. John Murray. 1910. p. 102.
5. *Hindu Manners, Customs and Ceremonies*: By Abbe A. J. Dubois. Translated by Henry K. Beauchamp. F.M.U. M.R.A.S., Oxford, Clarendon Press. Second Edition, 1899. p. 195.

Dubois brings out the fetish nature of the Egyptian animal worship. "The Egyptians considered that to kill, even by accident, one of their sacred animals was the most heinous of crimes. Whoever was guilty of such an act was invariably put to death. A Roman soldier was torn to pieces by the populace in spite of the terror that the name of Rome inspired, for having by mischance killed a cat. Diodorus, who records this incident, also mentions that during a famine the Egyptians preferred to deavour each other rather than touch the animal they held sacred." [1] Similarly, Francois Bernier, humourously draws a comparison between the Hindu religious belief of crossing the *Vaitarani*, that ghastly stream full of blood and carcases that separates the earth from heaven, with the help of a cow's-tail, and the Egyptian practice of crossing the Nile with the aid of the tail of a cow or a buffalo. [2] The sense of his statement is quite obscure and sarcastic. But this much is certain, as regards conscious imitation, the Zoroastrian has much in common with the inhabitants of Egypt that had gone before him as regards the special veneration towards the cow, and this seems to be the result of historical associations and conscious acceptance by the latter of the sociological traditions of the former.

In the Zoroastrian theory of cosmology, the bull enjoys the position of Adam as regards the animal world. From the bull sprang up all the other varieties of the

1. *Ibid.* pp. 195-196.

2. *Travels in the Mogul Empire*: By Francois Bernier. Translated by Archibald Constable. Second Edn. revised by V. A. Smith. Oxford University Press. 1914. p. 326.

animal kingdom. This is specifically stated in the *Zend-Avesta.* In the greater *Sirozah* the votary invokes the moon for the bestowal of the bull in all its ubiquity and plenty. "To the moon that keeps it in the seed of the bull; to the only created bull; to the bull of many species,"[1] we sacrifice. Again in the lesser *Sirozah*: "We sacrifice unto the moon that keeps it in the seed of the bull. We sacrifice unto the soul and Fravashi of the only created bull; we sacrifice unto the soul and the Fravashi of the bull of many species."[2] The presiding deity connected with the bull is the moon, the complacent bestower of happiness upon humanity, like the ungrudging services of the bull which meets their demands efficiently. The bull is the centre of the animal creation out of which are evolved all the different species on earth. *Pouru-Samedha Gaus* is the couple born of the seed of the only-created bull, and from which arose two-hundred and eighty species. The ox thus representing the first created animal species always exacted sympathy and veneration from those generations who lived in the infancy of world civilization and history, especially, more prominently the Iranian stock,[3] to whom it always appealed as the chief factor of their material plenty. Such is her potency and importance to the worshipper of Ahura Mazda that Ashi Vanguhi, the daughter of the Holy Mazda, "rich in all sorts of desirable things and strong"[4] declares to have hid "myself under the foot

1. *Sirozah.* I. 12, S. B. E. Vol. XXIII. p. 8.
2. *Sirozah.* II. 12 *Ibid.* p. 16.
3. Cf. Dr. A. A. MacDonnel: *A History of Sanscrit Literature.* p. 110. London. William Heinmann. (1905).
4. *Ashi-Yast*: 7., S.B.E. Vol. XXIII. p. 272.

of a bull walking under his burden "[1] to escape the cognizance of the Turanians who are pursuing her.

As regards her sacrificiol value, Zarathustra urges a strong admonition against the current debased practice of the offering of blood sacrifices by certain Iranian tribes to their various deities. "There, Verethraghana, made by Ahura, proclaimed thus : 'the soul of the bull, that wise creature, does not receive from man due sacrifice and prayer ; for now the Daevas and the worshippers of the Daevas make blood flow and spill it like water.' "[2] The *Daevas* of the *Avesta* are the exact opposites of the Sanscrit *Devas* and represent *Asuras* of heaven in ancient myths, and the evil genius and destructive element ever present on earth, when the passage is stripped of its allegorical tinsel. The soul of the ox does not receive due sacrifice and proper treatment. On the other hand it is immolated in sacrifices. This is sacrilegious, and the destruction of any living being is an injury to the *Drvaspa*. As regards the bloodless character of the Zoroastrian sacrifice much external evidence can be adduced, while the antagonism of Zarathustra towards the spilling of blood, in those early ages of element worship and crude ideas about ritual, is quite remarkable. This passage from the *Encyclopaedia of Religion and Ethics* [3] on Zarathustra and animal sacrifice is worth quoting, and brings out its prominent characteristics. " Just as *Haoma*-sacrifice conflicted with the

1. *Ibid.* 55. *Ibid.* p. 281.
2. *The Bahram Yast.* 54. S. B. E. Vol. XXIII. p. 245.
3. *Encyclopaedia of Religion and Ethics.* Vol. XI. 1920. Article on Sacrifice, (Iranian), by E. Edwards. B.A., M.R.A.S., p. 19,

distinctly ethical character of the prophet's reform, so also did animal sacrifice conflict with the highly spiritual conception of God to which he attained. We are prepared, therefore, to learn that under his influence the practice was discontinued, and the emphasis on ritual generally was greatly reduced. Plutarch was undoubtedly right when he said that Zarathustra taught the Persians to sacrifice to Ahura Mazda 'vows and thanksgivings'. Even Anahita, who, according to the *Yashts*, was honoured by all her devotees with 100 stallions, 1,000 oxen, and 10,000 sheep was invoked by Zarathustra with no animal gift. But after the death of the prophet —how long we cannot say—and with the return of the old nature-worship, the custom of sacrificing animals returned, just as did the practice of preparing and drinking the *Haoma*-juce at the service." This is in entire agreement with the findings of Darmesteter as quoted above.[1] At the same time, the *Zend* specifically mentions Ahura Mazda offering up a sacrifice "with haoma and meat, with bersema, with the wisdom of the tongue, with holy spells, with the words, with the deeds, with the rightly spoken words."[2] The special stress of Plutarch's description of the Zoroastrian sacrifice as being 'vows and thanksgivings' is pretty plain. Can the inclusion of *Haoma* and meat be an interpolation at a latter date, as we have seen above?

Another passage in *Zend-Avesta* is worth cognizance in this respect.[3] "The place in that house where of

1. *Ante.* pp. 77-78, S. B. E. Vol. IV. p. lxiii.
2. *Aban Yast.* 17. S. B. E.' Vol. XXII. p. 57.
3. *Fargard.* viii. 5. S. B. E. Vol. IV. p. 96.

the ground is the clearest and driest and *the least passed through by flocks and heards,*[1] by the fire of Ahura Mazda, by the consecreted bundles of barsema, and by the faithful " is the fittest place for the tentative disposal of the dead. Leaving aside the issue of the cleanliness aimed at, this passage may go to corroborate the idea we get about the blood-less character of the ancient Zoroastrian sacrifice, as we are supposed to assume that the sacrificial victims, which are always holy, would have been more acceptable to the deity and hence quite libertine until the last unit of breath leaves its body. But here we are warned against the selection of any particular part of the house which is defiled by the breath of flocks or herds being selected for the interment of any corpse.

To the Indo-Iranian, the purficatory value of *Gomez* or *Nirang* (ox's urine) can never be minimised. Material uncleanliness, personal defilement, constitutional malady in fact, any corporeal blemish, either inherent or external, is capable of being purged through the instrumentality of the urine of the ox. There is a strange myth in Zoroastrian ritual " The storm floods that cleanse the sky of the dark fiends in it were described in a class of myths as the urine of a gigantic animal in heavens. As the floods from the bull above drive away the fiend from the God, so do they for man here below ; they make him free from the death-demon" (*Franasu*) and the death-fiend flees away hellwards, pursued by the fiend-smitting spell : 'perish thou, O *Drug*....... never more to give over to death the world of

1. The italics are mine.

the good spirit!' "[1] So in the mundane world the most potent instrument in cleansing the unclean is *Gomez*, the urine of the ox, which occupies the central position in the animal kingdom.

In the *Avesta* are to be found several passages where in revelations to Zarathustra from Ahura Mazda about the various processes of purification in which *Gomez* is the principal liquid to purge with. A cumbrous process of purification has been expounded with great minuteness, wherein the defiled person has to experience various washings with *Gomez* and water alternately. Zarathustra invokes:

"O Maker of the material world, Thou Holy One! Can man be made clean that had touched the corpse of a dog, or the corpse of a man?

"Ahura Mazda answered: 'He can, O holy Zarathustra'

"How so?

"If the *Nasu* has already been expelled by the corpse-eating dogs, or by the corpse-eating birds, he shall then cleanse his body with *Gomez* and water and he shall be clean."[2] "In case the *Nasu* (fiend) has not been expelled by the corpse-eating dogs and the corpse-eating birds, the worshippers of Mazda shall dig three holes in the ground, fill it with *Gomez*, and he shall thereupon *wash his body with gomez and not with water.*"[3]

1. S. B. E. Vol. IV. p. lxxv.
2. *Fargard*. vii. 35-37 *Ibid.* pp. 105-6.
3. The italics are mine. *Ibid*, 37. *Ibid*, p. 106.

The following is another significant passage [1] about the purificatory ceremonies which a woman delivered of a still-born child has to undergo, and at the present day, strange it may seem, the Parsee lady undergoes the same process even if a live-child has been born to her.

" O Maker of the material world, Thou Holy One! what is the food that the woman shall first take?

"Ahura Mazda answered: '*Gomez* mixed with ashes, three draughts of it, or six, or nine, to send down the *Dakhma* within her womb.

"'Afterwards she may drink boiling milk of mares, cows, sheep or goats, with pap or without pap; she may take cooked milk without water, meal without water and wine without water,'

"'O Maker of the material world, Thou Holy One! How long shall she remain so? How long shall she live on milk, meal and wine?

"'Ahura Mazda answered: 'Three nights shall she remain so; three nights long shall she remain thus on milk, meal and wine. Then when three nights have passed, she shall wash her body, she shall wash her clothes, with *Gomez* and water, by the nine holes, and thus shall be clean.' "

The above passage brings out the purificatory value of cow's milk to the followers of Zarathustra. The value of cow's milk in libations is ever stressed upon. Vafra Nuvaza of yore tormented by the strong fiend-smiter, Thraetaona, who flung him up in the air in the shape of

1. *Fargard*, vii. 61-65. S. B. E. Vol- IV pp. 91-92.

a bird, flew aimlessly for three days and nights without finding his way back home. In his utter despair he cries out to Ardvi Sura Anahita : " Ardvi Sura Anahita ! do thou quickly hasten helpfully and bring me assistance at once. I will offer thee a thousand libations, cleanly prepared and well strained, along with Haomas and meat, by the brink of the River Rangha, if I reach the earth made by Ahura and my house." [1]

Cattle are always held sacred by the Iranian stock and their descendants. Lifting of cows is a crime deserving of capital punishment and is a fitting quality of a ruffian who resembles an ungoldly Ashemaogha, [2] while the bull, in the light of our present enquiry, is to the Zoroastrian at once an object of material plenty and spiritual splendour.

1. *Aban Yast.* xvi. 63., S. B. E. Vol. XXIII. p. 69.
2. *Fargard.* v. 36-37. *Ibid.* IV. pp. 60-61.

CHAPTER VI.

THE SIKH VIEW-POINT.

THE view we obtain from an examination of the Hindu religious literature about the cow is corroborated strongly by the Sikh outlook respecting the sacred character of the bovine species. Even at the present day, despite all the transforming influences highly rampant in a materialistic age, the Sikhs stand out as the prominent protagonists in the cause of cow-protection. The simple Jat peasantry much noted for their husbandry in the bounteous tracts watered by the *Panch-Ap*—the Five Rivers, through a process of harmless proselytisation by their patriotic and statesmanlike sacred Gurus turned out to be a militant fraternity of enthusiastic religionists. A succession of ten Gurus from Guru Nanak to Guru Gobind Singh, through a period ranging between the X and the XVIII centuries, reformed their religious creed and religious practices and crystallised all their tenets in the *Granth Sahib* which is the repository of the cardinal principles of the Sikh Religion.

Sikhism is at once a revolt against and a consummation of the Hindu Religion. It is a revolt against the much elaborated and unnecessarily drawn out phases of Hinduism, such as the predominant influence of the Brahmans and the invidious caste distinctions that followed in the wake of nascent Brahmanism of the earlier centuries of Aryan civilization which created unnecessary barriers between the different strata of Hindu society; the Hindu worship of idols which is not at all essential for a comprehensive understanding of God and the ultimate coalescence of the *Jiva Atman* with the Supreme Soul; the pliant attitude of the Hindus towards the aggressive evangelical spirit of iconoclastic outsiders, especially the Muhammadans. [1] In their revolt against Hinduism they reorganised and rejuvenated the otherwise backward and stagnant Jat peasantry. They reformed their religious creed, and simplified it. They abolished the compartmental system of the *Varna Ashrama Dharma* and the pretentious claims of the Brahmans. They equalised the different social strata and welded them together on a common plane into a patriotic band of enthusiasts bound by ties of fellowship and veneration to their Gurus. They trumpeted a loud protest against the Hindu practices of idol worship, altogether did away with it amidst great national dangers and ultimately proclaimed an era of simplified worship permeated to the core with faith, love and charity. Above all, the quiescent Jat of the former days was made a militant religionist ready to immolate his life in the cause of his religion. The *Sikh* or the disciple

1. Cf. "Sikhism as pointed out by Ibbetson and others was, like Buddhism twenty centuries earlier, a revolt against the pretentions of the Brahmans, the fetters of the caste system, and the exaggeration of the Hindu ritual." *Race Characteristics of the Punjab*. A paper read by Sir Michael O'Dwyer before the Royal Society of Arts (Indian Section) in February 1926.

of the earlier centuries became the *Singh* or the lion of our own day. [1]

And yet Sikhism is in one way the fulfilment and crowning of all that is best in decadant Hinduism. Hinduism has had her own hey-day in the pre-Christian and the early *Anno-Domini* centuries. Throughout her flourish, Hinduism had the never-flagging support of the rulers of the state. Rather, *yedha raja tadha praja,*— the monarchs set the tune to religion. Buddhism with all its commendable elements struck the death blow to Hinduism during the six centuries that cover up either side of the birth of Jesus of Nazareth. With but slipshod flourishes under a Samudragupta here [2] and, later on, a Krishna Deva Raya and a Shivaji there, Brahmanical Hinduism entered upon a career of evil days. All the cherishings of the Brahmanical type of Hinduism were, as it were, totally obliterated. Then followed the parcelling of India in the seventh century into discordant

1. Guru Govind, the last and greatest guru, of the Sikhs, himself declares about Charan Pahul. "I now institute the custom of baptism by water stirred with a dagger and change my followers from Sikhs (disciples) into Singhs (lions)". Quoted by Sir Michael O'Dwyer. *Op. Cit.* Cf. the ceremony of *Charan Pahul* instituted by Guru Gobind and its admirable description by General Sir John Gordon. K.C.B. *The Sikhs.* William Blackwood, Edinburgh. 1904. pp. 36-54.

2. In spite of their leaning towards Buddhism the Gupta kings may be said to be the champions of the Brahmanical form of Hinduism. ". . . . . the matter may be summed up in the remark that coins, inscriptions and monuments agree in furnishing abundant evidence of the recrudescence during the Gupta period of Brahmanical Hinduism at the expense of Buddhism." Smith: *Early History of India.* IIIrd. Edn. (1914) p. 303. Brahmanical Hinduism of the orthodox type may be said to be the official religion of Chandra Gupta Vikramaditya and Samudra Gupta. *Ibid* pp. 292 and 303 respectively. The Brahmanical influence upon Krishna Deva Raya and Shivaji is too obvious to need comment.

principalities under incompetent potentates often at war with each other and courting mutual ruin. The Muhammadan invasions followed next. The flagrant vices of society flourishing in an age of misrule consequent on an era of indifferent and highly irresponsible rulers were given another swing in their striking yet ephemeral somersaults. The flames of the Muhammadan invasions consumed before them all the flower of the Hindu race, the genuine religious and political stalwarts of the country. The surviving black sheep in the flock, of mediocre talents and of a highly mean order, pushed their claims to the fore-front and during their careers of personal aggrandisement they swept away the still remaining little good in Hinduism. At the opposite end, there is the other consuming torch of the deliberate translation into practice of the Muhammadan evangelical spirit. Out of these circumstances,—this pestle and mortor experiment, the Sikhs emerged glorious, rejecting all that is noxious and assimilating the yet remaining Aryan vestiges of decadant Hinduism. In this respect the Sikhs are at once members within the pale of Hinduism proper and yet outside it. Their God is of the type of the Hindu God,—a personal, masculine and highly paternal God. Their attitude to life is greatly in assonance with the Hindu one. Their customs and manners are totally like those of their Hindu brethern. Neither subordination under an alien conquering nation, nor continued mingling with the Muhammadans produced what Herbert Spencer would call "superorganic evolution", [1] the influence of environment and association

1. Herbert Spencer: *Principles of Socialogy.* London. Williams and Norgate. 1904. Vol. I. p. 4.

upon human life and make them show at least a faint leaning towards the religion of their aggressive neighbours. And the partiality towards the cow is one of the distinctly Aryan elements in their religious creed,[1] and, in this respect, with which we are at present mostly concerned, is their indebtedness to Hinduism quite marked and most important, while kine-killing is one of the stock missiles in the armoury of the Muhammadan creed to pick up a quarrel at a moment's notice with the Sikhs who resented it wholeheartedly and strained every nerve to prevent it, which ultimately resulted in the shaking to the foundations of their *Khalsa* and ultimate subjugation with but few felicitous moments under a Ranjit.

As has been pointed out above, the partiality of the Sikhs towards the cow is a heritage from the Hindu religious practices ever current in India. The bountiful nature of the cow, her "undefinable majesty of mein"[2] and innocent looks, her fundamental importance to agriculture, above all, her exalted place in almost all the ancient civilizations, Egyptian and Aryan, Buddhist and Zoroastrian have had their impressionistic effects upon the Sikhs. In this respect they are *sanatanists*, meticulous preservers of all that is good in the ancient religious practices of the Aryans.

1. Cf. Sir Michael O'Dwyer: "but he [Nanak] accepted the Hindu veneration for the cow (of which the Sikhs of to-day are the stoutest champions) and the Hindu doctrine of transmiragration, as the means by which the soul became purified so as to join its Maker." *Race Characteristics of the Punjab.* A paper read before the Royal Society of Arts (Indian Section) in February 1926.

2. *Beast and Man in India.* By John. Lockwood Kipling, C.I.E, Macmillan & Co. 1892. Second Edn. p. 115.

It may be difficult to find specific verses in the *Granth Sahib* about the absolute sanctity of the cow and the inexorable nature of the *upapataka* which shrouds the man who perpetrates the crime, of cow-killing as Manu would enjoin it. [1] Avowed declarations of the type we find in the Hindu sacred literature may be said to be almost absent in the sacred book of the Sikhs. Their veneration towards the cow is a legacy of the past—the bequeathed traditional attitude of the Aryans. The very historical settings of the Aryan social practices and their seemly sanctity appealed most to the Jat peasantry. Hindus as they originally were, they staunchily embraced and preserved them intact even after they turned neophites to the Sikh religion which is out and out a movement towards reducing to the minimum all religious and ceremonial practices.

In these circumstances we cannot afford to have any detailed and graphic account of the Sikh outlook towards the cow owing to the paucity of material at our disposal. Our observations consequently lose their static character since we have only to glean information from several stories preserved in the *Granth Sahib* and local traditions about the lives lived and the ways practiced by the Sikh Gurus, *Masands* and other seers, and from conclusions therefrom. Personal aencdotes of a trifling character, such as, a few *Masands* along with Nam Dev attending the *Id* festival at Lahore where an ox is to be sacrificed, or Muhammad Bin Taghlak ordering Nam Dev to reanimate a specially slaughtered

1. *Laws of Manu.* Translation by Georg Buhler. S.B.E. Oxford 1886. Ch. xi. verse 60.

cow failing which he must either abjure his religion or stake his life as penalty, throw side lights about the relations between the Sikhs and Muhammadans, and the importance of the problem of cow-protection for the Sikhs, which supplied the bone of contention for the two preeminently warring and martial people of the East. Thanks to Max Arthur Mecauliffe for his important work on *Sikh Religion*,[1] much of the local tradition which is of perennial interest to the student of Sikh religion and which would otherwise have been lost, has been preserved for us. With great patience he has made an exhaustive collection of local tradition and with a sympathetic and appreciative bent of mind brought them forth in a series of six volumes couched in an elegant style necessary for a readable narrative. Hc generous criticism and his collosal work are indispensable to the student of Sikh religion.

A proper understanding of the relationship between the Muhammadans and the Sikhs durings the memorable days of the development of Sikh religion alone will make us appreciate the import of the cow-problem to the Sikh religionist. The historical back-ground of medieval India had an ineffaceable effect upon the Sikh's constitution. Muhammadan hordes occupied the rich plains of Hindustan and made a permanant abode of India. The injunctions of the prophet Muhammad about the desirability and necessity of religious wars and the spreading of Islam at the point of the sword, is a ready weapon in the hands of the Muslim fanatic of the Medieval ages. The Afghan pedigree, the mountaineer's

1. *The Sikh Religion*: By Max Arthur Mecauliffe, in Six Volumes. Oxford. Clarendon Press. 1909.

hardihood, the flush of an immediate victory over the heterogenous mass of the Hindu population, the Muhammadan belief of finding a niche in the Muslim Walhala in sacrificing his life for the sake of religion and, above all, the injunctions of the Prophet, pushed the Muhammadan, even after he settled peaceably in Hindustan with the Hindu subjects as his neighbours, to pick up cause for quarrel with them, taunt them in all possible ways and finally make converts of them. The killing of the cows seemed to them the best method of teasing the Hindus.

On the other hand, the Sikhs were just then beginning their careers as reformers of the Hindu religion. They gradually became militant religious enthusiasts. It is within their very constitution that they are quite uncompromising as far as their religious creed is concerned. The cow is held sacred by them, while it turned out to be a supplementary tenet of Islam that cows must be killed whenever possible. The professors of both the religions tried to vindicate their individual convictions Sir Monier-Williams sums up the situtation in a most vigorous style:[1] "They [the Sikhs] even surpass the Hindu in some of his most inveterate superstitions; as for example, in ascribing divine sanctity to the cow. The killing of the cow is with the Sikhs, the most heinous of crimes,[2] meriting nothing less than capital punisment—not however from any injunction in the Granth, but from simple opposition to the

1 *Brahmanism and Hindusim*: By Sir Monier Monier-Williams. K.C I.E., London. John Murray. IVth. Edn. 1891, pp. 172-173.

2 In a foot note Monier-Williams adds that in the Punjab it was at one fine infinitely move criminal to kill a cow than to kill a daughter.

Musalmans, who, whenever they conquered any district peopled by Hindus, invariably slaughtered cows, both to ratify their victories and to show their contempt for Hindu superstitions." Out of this friction came out several interesting anecdotes concerning the supernatural powers brought to their aid by the Sikh *Gurus* and, religious seers to prevent cows from being slaughtered by the aggressive Muhammadan conquerer.

That the practice of sacrificing cows by the Muhammadans at their festivals is a late development cannot be denied. We will treat of it exhaustively when we consider the Muhammadan attitude towards cow-life. Here we will only touch the problem as far as the Sikhs are concerned. Rav Das whose hymns find a prominent place in the *Granth Sahib,* a contemporary of Kabir, the acclaimed saint of both the Hindus and the Muhammadans, in one of his hymns points out that cows were slaughtered by the Muhammadans at the *Id* and *Bakru Id* festivals. Speaking of Kabir's parentage, Rav Das Sings : [1]

> " He whose family used to sacrifice cows at the Id and Bakr Id,
> and who worshipped shaiks, martyrs and pirs,
> Kabir, the son of a father who used to do such things so succeeded that he became celebrated in the three worlds."

Again, the *masands* who went in search of Guru Har Gobind relate the reminiscences of their journeys and incidentally mention a particular anecdote concerning the *Bakra-Id* festival celebrated at Lahore. They point out that an ox was slain in commemoration of the intended sacrific of Ishmail by Abraham. [2] From these

1 Mecauliffe : *The Sikh Religion.* Vol. VI. pp. 340-342,
2 *Ibid.* IV. 156.

two anecdotes about the Sikh seers of the medieval India we can infer the fact that the Muhammadan practice of slaughtering cows at the *Bakra-Id* festival, comes into historical light during the early days of the Sikh religion.

The second point of note which is more important, is that some of the early Muhammadan conquerers of India were ever persistent in their policy of anti-cow preservation,—at least the most orthodox and conservative among them. As will be shown later on, there is no specific injunction in the *Qur-an* about the indispensability of cow-slaughter at the *Id* festival. Neither does Arabic practice show any slight similarity to the Muhammadan observances in India. The Muslims must find room to provoke their Hindu subjects and must make them proselytes to their faith. The killing of the cow is the only valve for them to touch upon. As an instance in point may be pointed out the ordeal meted out to the Sikh saint Nam Dev by Muhammad Bin Tughlak (1321-1388) well-preserved in Sikh tradition [1]

> "The emperor said, 'Ho, you Nama,
> Let me see the deeds of your God.'
>
> The emperor had Nama arrested
> 'Let me see your God Vithal;
> Restore to life this slaughtered cow,
> Otherwise I will strike off thy head on the spot."
> 'Your majesty, how can that be?
> No man can reanimate what is slaughtered.
> All I can do would be of no avail;
> What God doeth taketh place'
> The emperor fell into a fashion,
> And set a huge elephant at Nama.
> Nama's mother began to cry.
> 'Why dost thou not abandon the God of the Hindus

1 Mecauliffe: *The Sikh Religion* Vol. VI. pp. 28-29.

And worship the God of the Musalmans?
Namedeo: 'I am not thy son, nor art thou my mother.
Eventhough I perish, I will sing God's praises.
The elephant struck him with his tusks.
But Nama was saved by the protection of God.
The King said, 'The Qazis and the Mullas salute me.
But this Hindu trampleth on my honour.'
The Hindus said, 'O king, hear our prayer;
Take Nama's weight in gold.'
'If I take a bribe I will go to hell;
Shall I amass wealth by abandoning my faith?'
While Nama's feet were being chained
He sang the praises of God and beat time with his hands.
The Ganges and the Jumna may flow backwards,
But Nama will repeat God's name.[1]
When seven gharis were heard to strike,
The Lord of the three worlds had not yet arrived.
God afterwards came mounted on His garur,
Which beat the air with its wings.
He took compassion upon His saint
And came mounted on His garur,
Say but the word and I will turn the earth on its side:
Say but the word and I will upturn it altogether,
Say but the word and I will restore the cow to life,
So that every one may behold and be convinced.'
Nama said, 'Spancel the cow.'
They put the calf to her and milked her.
When the pitcher was filled with the milk the cow gave,
Nama took and placed it before the emperor,
And the time of trouble came on him,
He implored Nam Dev through the Qazis and the Mullas
'Pardon me, O Hindu. I am thy cow.'
Nama said, 'Hear, O monarch,
Hath this credential been exhibited by me?
The object of this miracle is,
That thou, O emperor, shouldst walk in the paths of truth and humility.
Nam-dev, *God* is contained in everything.
The Hindus went in procession to Nama,
And said, 'If the cow had not been restored to life,

1 Nam Dev got orders from the Emperor to restore the cow within a pahar or watch of three hours or suffer death. When seven of the eight gharis of the pahar had elapsed and the cow was not reanimated, Nam Dev felt anxious; but when the eighth ghari was struck, it is said God presented Himself and wrought this miracle to preserve His saint from the Emperor's wrath.

People would have lost faith in thee.'
The fame of Nam-dev remained in the world;
He took saints with him to salvation.
All trouble and sorrow befell the revilers
Between Nama and God there is no difference."

Besides the striking nature of the miracle related, this passage impresses in copious detail the general attitude of the average Muhammadan to the problem of conserving kine-life, even though there are illustrious exceptions like Babar, Akbar and even Aurangzib as we shall see in the chapter on the History of Cow-protection in India. The circumstances of the case point to the fact that this ordeal invented by that notoriously schemin monarch is not the outcome of his inquisitive or playful propensities but the result of deliberate political considerations. Nam Dev, performing several miracles, like the one quoted at length above, traversed throughout the length and breadth of Hindustans making several conversions; and in one of his religious tours he reached Benares. Muhammad Bin Tughlak alarmed at the influence of Nam Dev over his country-men, and fearing lest his inordinate influence should result in a general insurrection against his rule already rendered notorious for several impolitic and highly unsound projects, resolved to arrest him. As a plausible pretext for his intended arrest, he harped upon the Muslim's stock lyre of cow's-life. The sequel to the ordeal is quite plain; the exaltation of Nam Dev in the eyes of the people at large.

The hostility of the Sikhs towards the Muhammadan conquerors of India is quite marked. They are the preeminent protagonists in the cause of preserving cow-life, while the Muhammadans always stood, only after they set foot on the soil of India, as the avowed and wanton hunters after the life of the bovine species. This naturally resulted in a great friction, when ultimately the more numerical of the two contending races triumphed over the other, and thus the elimination of the Sikhs as a ruling nation is to be accounted for.

It is curious to note that the first and sixth Gurus of the Sikhs are a little indifferent towards the killing of life. In reality, Guru Nanak attaches some importance to the distinction between lawful and unlawful food. Guru Nanak sings : [1]

> " Nanak, let others' goods be to thee as swine to *the Musalman* and kine *to the Hindu* ;
> Hindu and Musalman spiritual teachers will go bail for thee if thou eat not carrion.
> Thou shalt not go to heaven by lip service ; it is by the practice of truth thou shalt be delivered.

Un-lawful food will not become lawful by putting spices therein. But an incident in his life which comes down to us shows that he is slightly indifferent towards killing life and taking flesh. Once he was on a tour to the religious fair at Kurkhetar near Thanesar in the present Ambala District. A disciple offered him a deer and, being exhausted, Guru Nanak cooked it for a repast. The Brahmans raised an uproar. And Guru Nanak repudiated this horror in a long hymn well preserved in Mecauliffe's work. [2] Guru Nanak argues that everything emanated from flesh, the life's organism and its sustaining stamina. Life is ubiquous, and to drink water is to eat flesh. In this manner to partake of the

1. *The Sikh Religion* : Vol. I. p. 33.
2. *Ibid.*, pp. 47-49.

vegetable kingdom is to kill life. Perhaps, Guru Nanak anticipates here, in a faint degree though, our Sir J. C. Bose !

But the case of Guru Har Gobind is on a different footing altogether. Baba Gurditta, the Guru's son, once went a-hunting. One of his followers out of mistake shot a cow for a deer. The cowherds made a huge clamour and out of compulsion he was forced to reanimate the cow. This was heard by his father who got quite cross and exclaimed : "It is not quite pleasing to me that any one should set up as God's equal, and restore life to dead." [1] Thereupon, Baba Gurditta offered himself up as a sacrifice towards the expiation of his sin and thus met his death at a very tender age.

But the more positive side of the beliefs of the Sikhs is quite interesting. Ramanad charges his community with eating animal flesh. "Under the pretext of its being a sacrifice, man tasteth meat as if it were ambrosia, though it is a poison ; then the five evil passions appear and torture him." [2] Kabir is more explicit on this matter. His hymns are full of sagacity, but only given a religious colouring. He condemns the selfish and crooked devices of mankind. "Thou fasteth to appease God, yet thou destroyeth life to appease thy palate." [3] Here the reference is to the Muhammadan practice of offering up a sacrifice on the first day of the lent of Ramdan. Again, "Thou takest life and deemest it religious ; tell me, my brethern, what thou callest is

1. *Ibid.*, Vol. IV. pp. 220-21.
2. *Ibid.*, p. 89.
3. *Ibid.*, p. 211.

religious."[1] He urges the advisability of personal sacrifice and signs :[2]

> "Kabir if thou desire the Beloved, cast off thy head and make it into a ball ;
> While palying attain such a state of *ecstacy* that *thou shall be satisfied* with whatever happeneth thee."

In the hymns of Guru Arjan the gifts of *kamadhen* or celestial cow which is bounteousness incarnate are extolled highly. Thus the hymn runs :[3]

> "As if a spancel were put on an ox to milk him ;
> As if a man were to mount a cow and chase a lion.
> As if one were to worship a sheep instead of the cow Kamadhen, which granteth all desires."

Again :

"The singing ot God's praises is as *the gift of* Kamadhen."[4]

The general attitude of the Sikh community towards the cow is one of reverential awe. Any attempt towards infringing upon its sacredness demands from them the strongest of remonstrances and they would stake their lives to make the life of the cow inviolate.

1. *Ibid.*, p. 247.
2. *Ibid*, p. 315.
3. *Ibid.*, Vol, III. p, 148.
4. *Ibid..* p. 204.

CHAPTER VII.

THE MUSLIM OUTLOOK.

THE problem of cow-protection in India will be solved, if the Hindu and the Muhsmmadan attitudes regarding the same are reconciled to each other. That the cow as a species occupies a prominent position in the light of almost all the religions and civilizations of the world is an established fact. It remains to be seen whether the religion of Prophet Muhammad, peace be upon him, has anything to say for the preservation of the bovine species on earth. If it does not positively ordinance any respect towards the cow, at least, has the *Qur-an*, as the average Muhammadan would lose no time in asserting, any categorical injunction to the effect that cows *must* be offered in sacrifice at the *Bakra-id* and other festivals ? Popular belief and general ignorance have done immeasurable harm to communal still-waters in India at the present day, as this fundamental religious dogma is shrouded with the misty sereen of the unknown, which the layman cannot dispel rationally but has capacity enough to assert something that springs up to his brain in defence of his theory of the indispensability of cows for sacrificial purposes. He takes initial pride in victimising a cow on every possible occasion and that too in the face of his neighbours. This is not at all any unqualified impeachment of the Muslim practices in India. Instances of a far more liberal and exalted kind, wherein prominent Muhammadans that claim India as their mother-country, that take it at least as a privilege to belong to this land of many creeds, have left their firm foot-prints on the sands of Indian History, as having striven to respect the feelings of their one-time subjects and neighbours, and spare the cow invariably at sacrificial functions.

But the problem is mainly concerned with the generality of the Indian Muslims—with the proletariat. The gulf between the *bourgeoise* and the intelligentia is very wide. The cultured few of both the communities, Hindus and Muhammadans, can well understond the real bearings of the issue, and can accommodate a policy of give and take and of mutual tolerance. While the masses are not in a position to reciprocate any concession towards the sentiments of the Hindus, they bring in the other issue of music before mosques and complicate it with the main issue of cow-protection in India. This complication of issues has of late caused much bad-blood between the two prominent communities of India, and invariably all the communal riots, to which we are at present forced to be sorry witnesses, owe their beginnings to either of the above mentioned issues. Excesses have been committed on both sides, much innocent blood has been spilt unecessarily, great destruction of property has taken place, and national prestige has been irretrievably lowered. Behind all this undesirable heap of superstition and bigotry, there is the problem of cow-protection. The problem is capable of being solved in no time, provided the requisite amount of cool-mindedness, rationality and reciprocity is forth-coming on the part of our Indian Muhammadan neighbours.

As Lord Meston rightly observes:[1]. " . . . . if there is any doctrine in the Hindu faith which knows no compromise, it is the sanctity of the cow. It comes down from earliest ages, when the cow was the closest friend of our common forefathers, the progenitors, though I suppose we must no longer call them the Aryan progenitors, of Hinduism; and it is intertwined with the heartstrings of the Hindu peasantry to-day. By a perversity which is not wholly accidental, the Moslems of Northern India have fixed on the cow as the only animal which it is fitting to slaughter, and to slaughter in considerable numbers, on a particular occasion in each year. The occasion celebrates the interrupted sacrifice of Isaac by his father Abraham on Mount Moriah: and in the other Islamic countries camels, sheep or goats are slain in the commemoration. In India the cow has become the favourite victim, partly for economic reasons for which I need not detain you, but partly also, I am afraid, *because of the distress which it causes to the Hindus.* It is impossible for us to assess the depth of the cumulative animosity generated from these two causes. It flares out every now and then in savage sporadic violence, which leaves trails of bitterness behind. It is true that the more enlightened men on both sides deplore the situation, but they cannot avoid being dragged in when trouble comes. At present their chief endeavour is to prevent ourbursts of

1. *The New Constitution of India*, being three Rhodes Lectures by Sir Courtenay Ilbert, and three by Rt. Hon. Lord Meston, delivered at University College session (1921-1922) of the London University. pp. 175-177. University of London Press. 1923. The Italics are mine. The second cause referred to by Lord Meston is the Muslim hatred of idolatory.

fanaticism from breaking the ranks of reform, and the restoration of order is left to the British administrator. But the more the responsibility devolves on the people themselves, the more urgent will it become to find a remedy for this evil in Indian life. When a remedy is discovered, and not till then, will it be possible to dispense with communal representation and its attendant ills."

The issues of the problem are clear and are to be seen on the surface. Is there any injunction in the *Qur-an* about the requisiteness of cows being slaughtered on sacrificial occasions? What is the import of Arabic tradition on this point which is the sure guide to Indian Muhammadans? In case no ordination is promulgated in the *Qur-an*, about the indispensability of the cow for sacrificial purposes, and endorsed by Arabic tradition, what is the positive attitude of Islam towards cattle in general and the cow in particular? As a side issue, when and where is to be located the genesis of the practice of slaughtering cows with special reference to India? What are the practical aspects of cow-protection to the Indian Muslim of the present day in contrast to the historical antecedents and legacies supplied by the more liberal of the Muhammadan sovereigns of medieval India? How far does the problem partake of an economic character, and how can it be effectively met with at the present day? These are the lines of investigation proposed in this chapter. When these issues are clearly understood by the masses, and in the right perspective, then India need no longer apprehend any troublous current of agitation as the one at present throbbing the hearts of the more cultured and literate sections of both the communities. We will now take up the issues one by one and examine their bearings in their relation to Indian conditions.

It is the custom of the day among the Muhammadans to assert that cow-killing is an article of faith as far as the type of Islamic sacrifice is concerned. But it will be apparent even to the most orthodox of Muslim theologians that Prophet Muhammad had not a word to say about the utter indispensability of cow-slaughter for sacrificial purposes. Slaughter of animals so far as the ritual of a religion is concerned, is the concomitant of sacrifice. But, strictly speaking, there is no provision for sacrifice in the Islamic creed. Even though the sense of sin and the need for atonement are strongly felt by the pious Muslim, they are not associated with any shedding of blood. Unlike other Semetic races, Islam emphasises the importance of pious deeds and charity in the expiation of sins. The Semetic beliefs in the sacredness of blood; the surrendering of less valuable things in the hope of attaining better desires; the efficacy of self-inflicted penalties in the shape of sacrifices; the instinctive offering of some of their belongings to commemorate a happy occasion such as the birth of a child,—all of which partake of the nature of sacrifice may be said to be alien to the spirit of genuine Islam. [1]

Several theories have been forwarded towards tracing the origin of sacrifice. According to a Muham-

1. *Encyclopaedia of Religion and Ethics.* Vol. XI. Art. *Sacrifice* (Muhammadan). p. 29.

madan writer [1] "sacrifice is as old as religion, because it has always been regarded as an act of religious worship. It is an acknowledgment by man of the kinship of the God he worships, a thanks-giving for blessings received, and, in course of time, it became an act of supplication for new blessings." Being coeval with the birth of religion, like religion in its initial stages, sacrifice was remarkably simple. From the burning of incense and perfumes, sacrifice gradually passed through the successive stages of offering frankincense, libations, and firstlings of shepherds [2] until it assumed the state of what Dr. Sylvain Levi [3] would call that of "savage realism" in which consecrated animals are regularly slaughtered with its concomitant processes of ritual and other external manifestations of litany.

Prior to the birth of the Prophet Muhammad, Arabia was steeped in a semi-barbaric state of paganism, with heterodox beliefs localised in particular tribes which showed ample signs of diversity as regards faith, superstitions, customs and fetish worship. The Prophet Muhammad had to deal with, and bring about a revolution in, the existing order of affairs. As an illustration, which is only relevant to our present investigation, the pagan Arab had a partiality towards cattle, and several concessions were granted to them. Take

---

1. D. M. Sadiq. "The Origin and Development of Sacrifice." *Islamic Review.* Vol. VIII. June and July. 1920. Nos. 6 and 7 pp. 281-282.

2. Cf. *Ibid.* Vol. VIII. Nos. 8 and 9. August and September 1920. pp. 340. and 344. Article on "*Origin and Development of Sacrifice*" by Dudley Wright. Cf. The Old Testament. *Numbers* viii. 17.

3. *Doctrine Du Sacrifice Chez Les Brahmanas.* p. 9. (Paris 1898). Quoted in Rhys Davids; *Buddhist India.* pp. 240-41.

this verse from the *Qur-an.*[1] Prophet Muhammad declares: "And God has not ordained any Bahirah, nor Saibah, nor Wazilah, nor Hami, but those who misbelieve invent a lie against God, for most of them do not understand". Commenting upon this verse, Palmer points out[2] that "these are the names given to certain animals which were marked and allowed to graze at liberty. Bahirah was the name given to a camel which had ten young ones; her ear was then slit and she was turned loose to feed. When she died, her flesh was eaten by men only, the women being forbidden to touch it. There were, however, cases in which any she-camel was so called and treated. Saibah signifies merely a camel turned loose, her being so turned out was generally in fulfilment of a vow. Wazilah was a term applied to any cattle including sheep and goat, and generally, meant a beast which had brought forth a male and a female at the seventh parturition. Hami was a stallion camel, which, after begetting the young ones, was turned loose." As all these superstitious customs have in them some of the vestiges of pagan fetishism, and the prophet was forced to forbid them during his earthly ministry to the followers of *El-Islam*, the creed of "resignation" to the will of *Allah*.

But with all his positive hatred to the heterodox beliefs of paganism, prophet Muhammad showed equally positive discrimination in the selection of lawful and unlawful food, which is generally in favour of the preservation of cattle life. The prophet is more explicit about the

---

1. *Qur-an.* v. 102 Trans. by. E. H. Palmer. S.B.E. Vol. VI. p. 112.
2. *Ibid* I, foot-note.

rules of diet to be observed when on pilgrimage to the Kabaah. According to the *Qur-an*,[1] prophet Muhammad declares: "O! ye who believe! kill not game while you are on pilgrimage. . . . . Lawful for you is the game of the sea, and to eat thereof; a provision for you and for travellers; but forbidden you is the game of the land while ye are on pilgrimage". This passage brings out forcibly the explicit nature of the prophet's declarations about the ban on cattle life being taken especially on occasions of pilgrimage to the Kabaah. Prophat Muhammad would advice his com- to patriots prefer fish to flesh, for the obvious reason of the effects of climatic conditions on Arabia which lead to a scarcity of cattle. When cattle are destroyed in large numbers on occasions of pilgrimage, which mean a concourses of millions of votaries, the country would be denuded of its beasts of burden and of food.

With all the categorical emphasis of this ordination in the *Qur-an* animals were slaughtered in Arabia at least on one occasion. At the annual pilgrimage to Mecca, pilgrims resort to a huge sacrifice of camels, sheep or goats, according to the individual capacities of the votaries, in the valley of Mina in commemoration of Abraham's intended sacrifice of Ishmail in accordance with divine commands.[2] Prophet Muhammad himself declares at times in favour of sacrifice.[3] "O! ye who

1. S.B.E. Vol. VI. pp. 110-111. *Qur-an.* v. 95-100.

2. *Ibid.* p. lxxiv. Cf. M. A. Mecauliffe: *The Sikh Religion.* Vol. VI. p. 156, wherein it is stated that even Indian Muhammadans impute all sacrifice of animals at least duringd their careers as rulers of India, as commemorative of the intended sacrifice of Abraham.

3. *Qur-an.* v. 95. S.B.E, Vol. VI. p. 110.

believe! God will try you with some-thing of the game that your hands and your lances take, that God may know him who fears him in secret ; and who so transgresses after that, for him is grevious woe." As a special case the Prophet promulgates the injunction, that in case any one purposely slaughters animals while on pilgrimage, which is considered to militate against the law, [1] he should offer its equivalent " compensation " in sheep as an offering to the Kabaah, according to the judgment of two equitable persons, or he must offer in charity to the poor the emoluments of the sacrifice and, at least, must fast, as a manifestation of his desire for expiation. Then "God pardons byegones "[2] Prophet Muhammad himself was in the habit of distributing flesh among the poor. Especially, his love for Kadijah made him extol her virtues very often, even long after her death, and he would often kill a *sheep* and distribute its flesh among the poor in honour of her memory. [3]

Even though slaughter of animals was at times resorted to in Arabia, and even though Prophet Muhammad was distributing flesh on certain memorable occasions, we do not find even a single instance where a cow was offered in sacrifice or was required to be offered in sacrifice. We may search in vain the whole of the *Qur*-an for a passage mentioning the cow by name even. But the second chapter of the *Qur-an* goes under the caption of the " Chapter of the Heifer," wherein we find a reference to the cow.

1. *Ibid.* p. xvi.
2. v. 96. *Ibid.* p. 111.
3. *Ibid.* p. xix.

Qur-an ii. 62-68 and 88-90 relates the story of the sacrifice of the cow [1] offered by Moses as described in Deuteronomy xxi. 1-9 and Exodus xxxii. 20. The story is quoted by prophet Muhammad and the second chapter of the *Qur-an* is named after the cow, simply to exhort the faithful against unbelief and apostacy. The prophet of Islam absorbs this story as an illustration against heterodoxy and unfaithfulness which the Jews were guilty of in their relations with their prophet and leader Moses. Fearing lest disunion among the followers of El-Islam should lead to national disruption, Prophet Muhammad strikes a note of warning in clearly bringing home to his followers this piece of infidelitey of the Jews towards their master. But for this we do not find another reference to the cow in the whole of the *Qur-an*.

That the indispensability of the cow for sacrificial purposes is nowhere to be found in the *Qur-an* and that the popular belief among the Muslim population is not theologically provided for is established beyond doubt and is conceded by recognised Muslim Maulvis and political savants. Hakim Ajmal Khan, a Maulvi of no mean scholarship, admirably reviewed the position of the cow in Muslim theology and ritual in his presidential address to the All-India Muslim League assembled at Amritsar in 1919. [2] The learned Hakim says: " we are, and should be fully cognizant of the fact that cow-killing seriously

1. *Ibid*. pp. 9-10 and 12-13.

2. *Hindu Muslim Unity*, comprising the presidential address of Hakim Ajmal Khan to the All-India Muslim League. Amritsar (1919), published as a pamphlet by the Cow-Protection Society, 43 Banstolla Street, Calcutta, and supplied to me by the courtesy of the Cow Preservation League, 171/A Harrison Road, Calcutta along with other statistical information.

annoys our fellow-countrymen. But before holding out any assurance to them, we must first see in what light our religion views this question. We must also determine the extent to which *Qurbani* is enjoined upon us irrespective, of course, of the slaughter of cows. According to Islam, *Qurbani* or sacrificial offering, is only *sunnat-i-muwakkidah* (a practice observed by the Prophet and emphatically enjoined on his followers) which Mussalmans as Mussalmans, as long as they can afford it, must observe. Now it is a matter of choice to fulfil this observance by sacrificing camels, sheep, goat or cow, which simply means that any of these animals can be fit offerings. Crores of Indian Muslims must be strangers to the slaughter of camels, for the fulfilment of this observance, but none of them can possibly be accused of the slightest religious omission. On the contrary, Mussalmans of Arabia, Syria, Egypt, Tripoli and Asiatic Turkey have been faithful to this observance without ever having slaughtered a cow, and I am confident no erudite theologian or *Mufti* can maintain that these Mussalmans have failed to observe the *Sunnat* (practice of the Prophet) or have been guilty of any religious shortcoming. If any Mussalman dares to call a religiously legitimate practice illegitimate he certainly commits a sin. I consider it appropriate at this stage, to recount some of the *Ahadees* (religious practices), according to which the sacrifice of animals other than the cow is entitled to preference. For instance, Ummti Salmah (the Holy Prophet's venerable wife) says that the Prophet once observed, 'if any of you see the Crescent heralding the month of Zil Hijjah and desires to sacrifice a goat . . .' etc., which obviously indicates that the Arabs were in the habit of sacrificing goats. According to another tradition, our Prophet said that of all sacrificial animals sheep was preferable ; if we reserve sheep alone for the offering, we will be complying with this tradition." He then exhorts the Indian Muslims to take the initiative instead of being advised by their Hindu neighbours, and by thus using judicious discrimination in the selection of the sacrificial animal which will be in best accord with Islamic tradition, bring about an era of peaceful relations within India and enhance national reputation abroad.

The trend of this exposition is amply corroborated by other statements of the Hakim Saheb again and again in the press and on the platform. Mr. Savel Zimmend, one of the prominent American visitors and sympathisers of India and her national aspirations, discloses the same confessions of Hakim Ajmal Khan, in the course of an article to the *New-York Times Magazine* [1] on the "Causes of Indian Disruption". According to Mr. Zimmend, the Hakim Saheb is declared to have said : "Bakra-Id is the religious festival in which Mussulmans perform their pilgrimages around their holy places in Mecca. At this festival they have to sacrifice in pursuance of the sacrifice of Abraham, the Mussulmans of India being too far away from Mecca go to the City of Ajmir. But neither the text of the Koran nor tradition enjoined the slaughter of a cow. In Turkey, Egypt, Syria and Persia where a cow might be slaughtered without offence to any-one, a sheep is preferred." Questioned about the reasons why the Indian Muslims prefer the cow to any other animal in their sacrifice, the Hakim continues: "Simply

[1] Reproduced in the *Hindu*, Madras, November 11, 1924.

because the goat and the sheep are much more expensive in India than the cow, and the Mussulman cannot afford the price of a sheep. *But the Koran specifies that the sacrifice is not necessary for the poor.*[1] Mussulmans are so poor that they cannot afford even a cow." The poor Muslims resort to the sacrifice of cows "because all people are not actuated by common-sense and good feeling." These two extracts practically conclude that neither *Qur-an* nor Arabic tradition has anything to say about the fundamental importance of cow-slaughter in Islam on sacrificial occasions.

Here we must not omit noting the influence of climatic conditions upon the social practices of the Arabs in respect of sacrificial offerings. The regional configuration and the influence of atmospheric conditions render scarcity of cattle, especially of the bovine species, a corollary of Arabian life. Chronic state of poverty attendant upon a region of deserts and draughts, and scarcity of pastures and dearth of cattle, rendered the position of the Arabs quite intolerable. Even if they had very strong notions about sacrifice and its efficacy in obtaining atonement, they could not have effectively got through their objects, handicapped as they were by poverty and scarcity of cattle. This was why Prophet Muhammad declared in favour of the "game of the sea" and prohibited resort to the "game of the land" on occasions of pilgrimage[2] for the obvious reason of the scarcity of cattle, as we have already seen above. This

1. The Italics are mine.
2. *Qur-an.* v. 95-100., S. B. E. Vol. VI. p. 111.

is admirably summed up by Mr. Weir. [1] He observes: "Animal sacrifice could arise and continue only in a country rich in pasture, where a sheep or even a camel could be easily spared; but in Arabia, if we leave out of account the south-west corner, the whole population outside the towns has always been in a chronic state of semi-starvation. So poor were the Arabs that up to the time of Muhammad they were in the habit of burying their female infants, nominally for the fear lest they should, by capture or otherwise, bring dishonour upon the tribe to which they belonged, but in reality because they had not the means of supporting them. The ordinary food of the desert Arab consisted of the dates and the milk of camels when available, and, when his inveterate hospitality did lead him to the lavish slaughter of his beasts, every particle that could be eaten was consumed, if not by himself and his guests, by the destitute women and children who hung about his tent, so that not much was left for the dogs."

It will be plain by now that the Arabian customs of sacrifice were not as lavishly indulged in as the Brahmanical ones in India. Cattle were not enough and to spare in Arabia. Even when the Arabs improvised means to carry through a sacrificial ceremony, only a sheep or a goat and in some cases a camel too, was preferred as they only were available in the country. Cows were not easily procurable, and, even when capable of being procured were not sacrificed in countries like Egypt and Palestine which were more favourably and richly

1. *Encyclopaedia of Religion and Ethics* (1920). Vol. XI. p. 29. Article on *Sacrifice* (Muhammadan) By T. H. Weir. Glasgow University.

endowed with the bounties of nature. Their partiality for camels was quite marked, and the social and economic structure of their body-politic left out of their purview any infringement upon bovine cattle, even when they were available.

From this we are led to ask, where and when are we to locate the genesis of cow-slaughter in Muslim sacrifices, and what are the antecedents to the prevalence of those practices ? History points out to the fact that the practice of the slaughter of cows in India is traceable only to the times following the Arab conquest of Sind in the early decades of the eigth century of the Christian era, and the inroads of Muhammadans hordes which were ultimately instrumental in swallowing up the disintegrating empire of Harsha-Vardhana. As we have already found out, slaughter of cows is nowhere to be seen in the regularly Muhammadan countries of the so-called Middle East, whereas we find several instances where cows were slaughtered by Muhammadans after they set foot on the Indian soil. From this we are to conclude that the slaughter of cows for sacrificial purposes is only a later development of Islamic ritual and usage coming into prominence during the period of the Muslim conquest of India.

Historical evidence from contemporary sources is not wanting to substantiate this thesis. Kalhana Panditha mentions in his *Rajatarangini*, one of our first regularly historical documents, that the Lavanyas being vanquished by Harsha (1089—1101), one of the kings of Kashmir, "ate cow's meat at the hands of the *mlechchas*." [1]

---

1. *Rajatarangini*. vii. 223. Translated by Dr. M. Aruel Stein. Vol. I p. 465.

The *mlechchas* referred to are the Muhammadans whom we meet under the same appellation in almost all our ancient documents, whereever they are mentioned. The Muhammadan appetite for beef *must* have originated only after they set their foot on the soil watered by the *Panch-Ap*. The accuteness of the tension between the Hindus and the Muhammadans is clearly discernible when we come to the Muslim-Sikh struggle in the sixteenth and the following centuries. That the Muhammadan tenacity in declaring the indispensability of cows for sacrifical purposes is purely vindictive, we found out when we treated of the Sikh attitude.[1] Sivaji felt positive hatered towards the Muhammadan practices of slaughtering cows vindictively and in the face of the Hindus at Bijapur. This hatered, as preserved in the *Siva Digvijaya* may be pronounced to be the prominent incentive to all his patriotic struggles. [2] From this historical evidence it is practically established that the Muslim practice of slaughtering cows is a later development of Islamic ritual seeing its inception only after they set foot on the Indian soil.

How this change was brought about is our next problem. Besides the one pointed above, the main reason is to be found in the general ignorance of the masses and the misunderstanding and confusion of thought as regards the Arabic and Urdu words for goat

1 *The Sikh Religion*, Vol. VI. pp. 28-29, by, M. A. Macauliffe. Cf. *Brahmanism and Hinduism*, pp. 172-173, by Sir Monier Monier-Williams, and Lord Meston's remarks quoted at the beginning of this chapter.

2 *Siva Digvijaya*, p. III, Translated in part in *Siva Chatrapati* by Dr. Surendra Nath Sen, Calcutta University Press, 1920, p. 160.

and cow. This is purely a question to be decided by acknowledged linguists, and the generality of the Muhammadan commnnity cannot well understand it in all its bearings. Dr. Leitner writing in the *Asiatic Review* as far back as 1893 admirably brought out the fallacies of the prevailing dogma among the Indian Muslims. He says: [1] "The Hindustani name for goat is 'bakra', but the 'k' is a 'kef', whereas the 'k' in the Arabic word 'Baqr' or 'Bakr' is a 'qaf', but it makes all the difference to the peace of India if the 'Bakra-Id' is with a 'kef' or a 'qaf'. If it be, as the vulgar call it, and it is in general practice, 'a sacrifice of goats' or 'Bakra-ka-Id,' or even 'Bakra-Id,' the contention between the Hindus and Muhammadans is at an end, but if, as mischief-makers have invented, 'baqr-Id' is a festival of the sacrifice of a cow, then the Pax Britannica may at any moment give way to a universal rising among the Hindus throughout India. *It is therefore the most elementary common-sense and good feeling which would point out to the Muhammadans that the sacrifice of a cow is not enjoined by the text or tradition regarding the festival,* [2]. But that on the contrary, it is universal as it most certainly is seditious in India. In Turkey, Egypt, Syria and Persia, where a cow *might* be slaughtered without the least offence to any one, a sheep is preferred; why then should a cow be killed in India, where it is a most heinous crime in the eyes of

1 *Young India*, January 7, 1920, article on *Qurbani and Hindu Muslim Unity* reviewing the address of Haziq-ul-Mulk Ajmal Khan. *Young India* from 1919-1922. Published by S. Ganesan, Madras, with an introduction by Dhirendra Nath Pal. pp. 407-408, foot-note. (1922).

2 The italics are mine.

the vast majority of the population, and when neither scripture nor pratice requires it throughout the Muhammadan world." If the Muslim population is made to realise the actual truth behind this prevailing confusion, the bad blood that had been generated between them and their Hindu neighbours, will in no time have been dispelled. This is our task at the present day.

The positive attitude of Islam and of Muslim tradition towards cow-life is quite remarkable in spite of all this heap of prejudice and ignorance. According to *Islami Gorakshan* [1] the prophet is said to have declared to his wife Ayesha: "Cow's milk is the chief cause of recovery and health. Ghee is a medicine and beef is a disease . . . . Cow's milk is the means to cure diseases. Butter is the medicine, flesh is the disease." The meaning of this tradition is pretty plain and points to the recognition by the prophet of the beneficient qualities of the products of the cow. According to another tradition of Islam, the earth is believed to be resting on one of the horns of a cow, which make us, Hindus, reminiscence the place of *Kamadhen* in Hindu mythology and belief. Ali, the son-in-law of the prophet, and Ghouse Azam, one of the prominent saints of Islam, never

1. *Islami Gorakshan*. pp. 31-32. A brochure written by the late Syed Nazir Ahmed Saheb, Vakil, Sitapur. U.P., and published by the Superintendent, Islami Gorkshan Office, Sitapur, U. P. (1925), and supplied to me by the courtesy of the Superintendent along with a short history of the Association. The problem of cow-protection from the Muslim view-point is admirable treated here.

It is my pleasant duty to acknowledge the help rendered to me by my friend *Afsa-Rush-Shora*, Mahomed Baig, *Jowhar*, Lecturer in Urdu, Noble College, Masulipatam, in translating this brochure from Urdu for me and thus facilitating my investigations, touched beef in their life-time, owing to their respect for life of the cow.

When we turn to the attitude towards cow-life of the more noble of the Muslim monarchs of India we find that they were actuated by feelings of sympathy and good-will towards the veneration of the cow by their Hindu subjects. Regal legislation in this matter is adduced in abundance from contemporary documents in the chapter on the history of cow-protection in India. But here we will only touch in outline the general trend in this respect of Muslim thought of the more exalted kind. Babar in his advice to his son Humayun exhorts him to befriend the Hindus and in particular protect the cow from slaughter. [1] The whole of his *Memoirs* may be read with zeal, but in spite of his descriptive detail, we find no mention of cows being slaughtered anywhere : on the other hand, he had a particular partiality towards camel's flesh.[2] Akbar's clemency towards and favour of his Hindu subjects is noteworthy. His *firman* to the Jains regarding the protection of cow-life, [3] his positive distaste for flesh

1 The original copy of the document is in the Bhopal State Library, and for the first time made available for the public by Dr. Syed Mahmud, Ph. D., in his article on Cow Production Under Muslim Rule, in *The Indian Review*, Madras, for August, 1925. This article as printed as a pamphlet for free distribution by the *Gorakshaka Mandali*, Chickpet, Bangalore.

2 *Memoirs of Babar*, Translated by Leyden and Erskine, Revised by Sir Lucas King, Oxford. 1921, 2 Vols. Vol. I, p. 281.

3 See the Introduction by S. N. Banerjee to *The Commentary of Father Monserrate*, p. v., Humphry Milford. 1922. Cf. *Bhandarkar Commemoration Volume*, pp. 265-265. Article on The Jain Teachers of Akbar, by V. A. Smith. Bhandarkar Oriental Institute, *Poona*, 1917.

and his injunctions towards total abstinence [1] show his farsightedness in endeavouring to bring about economic and social equilibrium in the realm. Francois Bernier informs us [2] that even Jehangir, who is a mixture of oddites, and frivolous in the extreme, and Aurangzib, falsely notorious for the persecution of his Hindu subjects, passed favourable laws towards the preservation of cow-life. In modern times, but for the exception of the recent *firman* of the Nizam of Hyderabad, [3] there is a univeral movement among the more liberal of the Muslim rulers to protect cow-life. Even the Amir of Afganistan prohibited cow-slaugter in his dominions in the year 1923. [4] This is the legacy of the Muhammadan sovereigns of India who were filled with more exalted views on social solidarity and economic stability of the country.

The question which remains to be considered is, what is the attitude of the generality of the Muhammadan population of India towards cow-protection, and how is it to be modified if found undesirable? In the light of our investigations so far worked out, chronic ignorance and popular prejudice has so jaundiced the outlook of the average Muslim that he cannot recognise the truths about cow-life from the genuine Islamic viewpoint as well as in the light of general tradition. He cannot look at the Hindu in the face. He would argue out that the slaughter of cows is simply resorted to from

1 *Ain Akbari*. p. 56. Translated by Francis Gladwin.

2 *Travels in the Mogul Empire*. pp. 326-27.

3 Quoted *Ante*. Introduction. p. 8n.

4 *Islami Gorakshan* p. 41.

economic stress. But he cannot realise the economic loss to the nation at large by way of the encroachment upon the bovine species. He would argue that the poverty of the Muslims is proverbial. The price of a goat or a sheep is prohibitory when compared with that of a cow. As such, a family of persons may with profit sacrifice a cow at a lesser cost than each member of the family sacrificing a goat or a sheep individually.[1] On the other hand, he would complicate the issue with the other one of Hindu music before mosques. The muddle looks so complex that we cannot in any way bring about an efficient solvent to remove existing undesirabilities.

In his presidential address at the Thirty-Eighth Annual Session of the Indian National Congress held at Cocanada (1923), Maulana Mahomed Ali brought out in clear terms the economic implications of the Muslim practice of beef eating.[2] According to this Muslim leader, Indian Muslims take to beef as an article of food only because they cannot afford to have mutton at a higher cost. His advice to the Indian Muslims would be:[3] "The only sure way of stopping cow-killing in this case is to take steps to lower the price of mutton which is prohibitively high, and thus reduce the very large margin that there is at present between the prices

---

1. Cf. *Encyclopaedia of Religion and Ethics.* Vol. XI. p. 31. Art. Sacrifice (Muhammadan). "Partnership in a sacrifice except between members of a family, is (by the Malekite School) forbidden in Islam."

2. *Presidential Address,* pp. 78-81. Aligarh, (1923.)

3. *Ibid.*, pp. 80-81.

of mutton and beef. I am far from desiring that the cost of living should be still further increased for any section of this impoverished land, not excluding my own community, which is admittedly one of the poorest; but I cannot help pointing out that by far the most numerous owners of cows are the Hindus, and that if they did not sell cows after they ceased to give milk, there would be much less cow-killing than there is to-day. Even now, we can encourage sheep-breeding in order to save the cow. . . . Nevertheless, I appeal to my co-religionists, even to-day, to discontinue the use of beef and not to wait until Swaraj is won when their sacrifice would be much less. The joint-family system of India, and not the free competition of the Manchester School must be our social and political ideal for India's different communities. But if there is to be competition between the different communities that form the Indian joint-family, let it be a competition in forbearance, self-sacrifice, and I maintain that the community which willingly surrenders more of its cherished rights and strongly entertained sentiments for the sake of sister communities and the peace and harmony of India, will prove the most invincible in the end." This is a highly practicable solution of the cow-problem and has all the force of convincing verity. Prominent Muslim patriots of India like Hakim Ajmal Khan, Maulana Abul Bari and Mian Chhotani have prevented cow slaughter and preached about cow-protection,[1] and India's national aspirations are centered in this class of our Muslim compatriots.

---

1. *Young India*, June 8, 1920. *Young India* (1919-1922) p. 411. Published by S. Ganesan, Madras. (1922).

NOTE BY[1]

Mr. MUHAMMAD MARMADUKE PICTHALL.

There is absolutely no Islamic order or tradition for the slaughter of cows at 'Id-ud-Dhuha' or at any other time. We had never heard of *cows* being regularly and habitually killed for food until we came to India. In other countries of Asia, and in Europe, where beef is eaten oxen and not cows are always kept for slaughter.

There is no institution of animal sacrifice in Islam, in the sense of propitiation or atonement. All the sacrifices of the pagan Arabs were converted by our Prophet into acts of charity. Animal food being the best and most nourishing food obtainable in Arabia, where the vegetation is generally of a kind which cattle can eat, but man cannot eat, he ordered that cattle should be slaughtered upon solemn occasions by men who could afford such charity, and that the meat should be distributed among the poor. The plea of poverty put forward by the ignorant Muslims as an excuse for slaughtering a cow rather than a sheep or goat takes them clean out of the category of those who are enjoined to 'sacrifice'. The yearly "Feast of Sacrifice" is not a feast of animal sacrifice as many people seem to think but the feast of the supreme sacrifice, the only sacrifice which God requires of man according to the teaching of the Quran and the Prophet —the surrender of man's will and purpose to the will and purpose of his Lord as illustrated in the sacrifice

1. Communicated to me by the courtesy of the manager, *Islamic Culture*, Hyderabad, in view of the fact that it was intended to be published by way of editorial note to the above chapter originaly designed to see light of day in that Journal.

of Abraham. It is in fact the festival of Al-Islam (which means that self-surrender). The slaughter of animals for food on that occasion is only in commemoration of the sacrifice which Abraham was told to make which marked a great event in human history—the end of human sacrifice for the Semitic race, ages before it came to an end among the other races of mankind.

ومن يرغب عن ملة ابراهيم الا من سفه نفسه ولقد اصطفيناه في الدنيا وانه في الآخرة لمن الصالحين

اذ قال له ربه اسلم قال اسلمت لرب العالمين

"Who will forsake the religion of Abraham save he who hath made himself a fool. We chose him for his goodness in this life and surely in the after life he is among the righteous."

"When his Lord said unto him: Surrender! he said: I have surrendered to the Lord of the Worlds."

The whole teaching of the Quran and the Prophet seeks to demonstrate to man's intelligence that this Surrender or Submission to the will and purpose of Almighty God as revealed in the Scriptures and manifested in creation, and not the recital of any creed or the performance of any rite, is Religion. When this is realised—and it is astonishing how many people fail to realise it—such passages of the Quran as verily "Religion with Allah is Islam," and "Whoso offereth a religion other than Islam, it shall not be accepted from him" (the usual translation) become "verily religion with Allah (consists in) the Surrender (or submission to His will and purpose)", and "Whoso offereth a religion without Surrender (or submission to God's will and purpose) it will not be accepted from him." They are at once changed from a sectarian statement to the statement of a universal truth. Those who think of our Feast of Sacrifice as a festival of the sacrifice of animals "forsake the religion of Abraham and have made themselves fools."

There is another aspect of Islamic teaching evident in the Quran and in our Prophet's teaching which we have never seen mentioned in connection with this controversy. To us it seems perfectly clear that the Quran teaches that the slaughter of animals for food is itself in the nature of sacrifice—the sacrifice of the lower order of life to the higher, or simply of the weaker to the stronger, which runs as a law through all animal existence. Our Prophet's kindness and concern for animals are preserved in many sayings and anecdotes, which merit more attention than has hitherto been given to them by the exponents of Fiqh, and in the Quran itself we read:

وما من دابة في الأرض ولا طائر يطير بجناحيه إلا أمم أمثالكم

ما فرطنا في الكتاب من شيء ثم إلى ربهم يحشرون

"And there is not an animal in the earth nor a flying creature flying upon wings but is a people like unto you. We have neglected nothing in the Book (of our decrees). Then unto their Lord they will return".

Man is held responsible to God for his behaviour towards these "peoples like unto ourselves", and therefore the slaughter of animals for food is a serious matter, undertaken only in obedience to divine command. Man has to remember God, that is his own subordinate position and mortality, when performing it, and also his own duty to sacrifice his life upon occasion. The words used in connection with the slaughter of animals for food in the Quran and Ahadith are always solemn words of religious association. This alone has led some people to imagine that animal sacrifice, for propitiation or atonement is perpetuated in Islam, which it is not.

We now come to the incident of the sacrifice of a Yellow Heifer alluded to by Mr. L. L. Sundara Ram in his article [sic. the above chapter.] It is thus described in the Quran :

وإذ قال موسى لقومه إن الله يأمركم أن تذبحوا بقرة قالوا أتتخذنا هزوا قال أعوذ بالله
أن أكون من الجاهلين

قالوا ادع لنا ربك يبين لنا ما هي قال إنه يقول إنها بقرة لا فارض ولا بكر عوان
بين ذلك فافعلوا ما تؤمرون

قالوا ادع لنا ربك يبين لنا ما لونها قال إنه يقول إنها بقرة صفراء فاقع لونها
تسر الناظرين

قالوا ادع لنا ربك يبين لنا ما هي إن البقر تشابه علينا وإنا إن شاء الله لمهتدون

قال إنه يقول إنها بقرة لا ذلول تثير الأرض ولا تسقي الحرث مسلمة لا شية
فيها قالوا الآن جئت بالحق فذبحوها وما كادوا يفعلون

"And (remember how) when Moses said unto his people, Lo! Allah commandeth you that ye sacrifice a cow, they answered: art thou making game of us? He said: Allah forbid that I should be of the foolish".

"They said: Beseech thy Lord for us that He make clear to us what (cow) it is. He answered: Lo! He saith verily it is a cow neither with calf, nor immature, she is between the two conditions, so do that which ye are commanded.

"They said: Beseech thy Lord for us that He make clear to us of what colour it is. He answered: Lo! He saith, verily it is a yellow cow, bright is its colour, gladdening beholders.

"They said: Beseech thy Lord for us that He make clear to us what cow it is; for cows seem all alike to us, and verily if Allah wills shall be led aright.

"He answered: Lo! He saith, verily it is a cow unyoked, that plougheth not the soil nor watereth the crops, sound and without blemish. They said: now thou comest with the truth. So they did sacrifice it, though against their will". The Israelites, who were the Muslims of those days, had become infected with the cow-worship which prevailed in Egypt, as is shown also by the incident of the golden calf—which no doubt represented the yellow heifer, the colour which they held as sacred. After the golden calf had been destroyed by Moses, the yellow heifer still existed and was worshipped by the people secretly. When taxed with their deceit, the people pretended ignorance, asked what cow was meant, what colour it was and so forth, and pretended that they made no difference between one cow and another. Moses drove the matter home, moreover, and in the end they had to slaughter it though much against their will.

The points to be noted here are that the creature that the Muslims were ordered to sacrifice in the time of Moses was one that they themselves, who knew better, had chosen to worship in place of Allah, not one which their neighbours worshipped in pursuance of another religion. The order was not given while they were in Egypt, as a challenge or affront to the cow-worshipping Egyptians, but when they were alone with their own Prophet in the desert wanderings. It was intended to purge the Muslim body of views obnoxious to Islam, not as a protest against views held by other people. It is therefore no precedent for the slaughtering of cows by Indian Muslims; but rather a precedent for the sacrifice or elimination of all institutions and personalities which the Indian Muslims have allowed to come between the individual worshipper and the One object of worship, and which have no right to exist in the Muslim brotherhood.

CHAPTER VIII.

THE HUMANITARIAN ATTITUDE.

IN this chapter we have to deal with the promptings of some of the finest instincts of man. Human sentiment is a complex of emotions each one trying to dominate the other. But, like the famous slogan of Rousseau,[1] that "man is born free, but every where is found in chains," it is counteracted by other co-existent emotions. Generally, we say, man has, a particular disposition. By this we do not mean that he is a slave to that particular aptitude or disposition. On the other hand, he only shows special leaning towards a certain prompting of the sensorial organism, levened with the influence of other sources of volition. What medieval physiologists call "humours", are simply dispositions pushed to one extreme. Thus, if a man is easily irritable without cause or provocation, he is said to have secreted a large quantity of bile in his liver. Likewise with other humours. In this complex of humours or, to use a more refined term, emotions, humanitarianism is one, and is more exalted than other sensory expressions.

Humanitarianism is, indeed, high sounding jargon. But when expressed in simple homely language it means merely kindness, sympathy, regret and relief. All these concepts put together will give us the real import of the word humanitarianism. It is born with man's appearance on earth. But an expression is given to it when an

---

1. Jean Jaques Rousseau: The very first line of his *Contract Social.*

outward agency ruffles it. Thus, when we see a particular live being tortured, or, for that matter, given cause of pain, certainly, something in side ourselves is pricked and we regret such an incident. Even we may go to the extent of cursing our lot for having been unwary witnesses to it. This is but a prompting of the humane element naturally present in the human constitution. Extinction of life is not absolutely necessary to ruffle this emotion of ours. It may happen, at times, that certain men are not at all moved at a ghastly incident at which other people shudder and collapse. As an instance, take the case of a butcher. Daily he slaughters animals by the hundred. It is as easy for him to slaughter a goat or even a cow, perhaps, not a human being, as you and I drink a cup of coffee or cross the street in front our doors. The executioner, likewise, deals with the lives of men. To this class of people, all their senses are deadened; and the growth of their humane instinct is stunted. These get so, out of profession or habit. There are cases possible wherein people do not feel the least distaste to face a tragedy and without being touched in their hearts. These people we brand as the hard-hearted. But take the butcher out of his profession and place him in another situation. Occasions need not be many to elicit from him a passing sigh and a tear of regret. Even with the hard-hearted man the case is not difficult. He will be stirred in his soul some time or other and will ultimately have an emptying of his heart. All men are blessed with this instinct of humanitarianism. But the difference is only one of degree and intensity. Family affection forms one of the generative sources of this instinct.

Generally, we speak that the benefits of humanitarianism, ought to be showered upon the animal kingdom, since unlike human sufferers they are not capable of speaking out their grievences and claim for charity. The animal having cause of pain must groan silently within itself and bear its wretched lot. On the other hand, unlike a suffering animal, man can make himself heard, and importunate his fellow human beings to commisseration. Supreme religion reminds us of this kind of charity, by adopting *Ahimsa Paramo Dharma* as its supreme motto. This is the creed of Mahaveera, Buddha and later on Asoka the *Raja Rishi.* This is the supreme ideal placed by the Buddha before humanity. The Jains stand at the present day as the supreme lovers of life and they feel the greatest compunction to injur even the lowest order of insects. The fine truths of religion,—every religion, embrace this wholesome attitude to God's creatures upon earth.

But in the ordinary functions of life, we find ourselves unwarily destroying life in greater of lesser magnitude. Especially, when we think of the major or bigger animals, we find that they are put to several injuries. When the cart-driver uses his whip, overburdens the animal and makes it travel long distances without sufficient recuperation given her by sufficient food, drink and rest, he is inflicting pain upon the animal. When the farmer twists the tails of a pair of bullocks to make them drag the plough, it is inflicting cruelty upon them. When an animal is neglected in case of ailment, with scalds on its back exposed to the tortures of the insect and the bird, it is sheer cruelty done to it without the positive instrumentality of man.

In the commisariat line, cattle are put to unspeakable worry and strain. Take this significant passage [1] from the pen of Samuel Phinsoll, M. P., referring to the export of cattle to foreign countries from England; "On several occasions I saw men pour paraffin oil into their ears, which, as soon as it reached their brains, caused the poor brutes to fairly shriek with pain. Occasionally the ears were stuffed with hay, which were then fired; while in many instances the tails were snapped in the endeavours of the cattle-men to force the animals, that had laid down from sheer exhaustion, to regain their feet. The Commander of the vessel was appealed to, in the hope that he would order cessation of these cruel practices. 'I am, however,' said he, 'powerless to interfere in this matter. My duties are simply to carry out the instructions of my employers, the cattle being regarded by me as freight, nothing else.' The reason that the animals, no matter how horribly inflicted, sick, or suffering, are not put out of their misery, is to be found in the imperative rules of the Insurance companies both of New York and London". Abuses like these are numerous and they need to be reduced to the minimum.

The supreme ideal for man is the creed of vegetarainism. The slaughter of animals has a demoralising tendency upon human feelings. As forcibly pointed out by Sydney H. Beard: [2] "The harm done to man's moral nature directly by the consumption of flesh and

1 Quoted in *The Cow-My Dumb Mother.* By Gundu Rao Khadre. Manager, *Sree Gorakshak Mandali*, Bangalore, pp. 12-13.

2. *Ibid* p. 23.

blood, is suggestive of the indirect evil which results from the barbarous practice. It is undeniable that where slaughter and bloodshed are most prevalent, people become brutalised and crime increases. In the east end of London, where slaughter houses are numbered by hundreds, where little children are sent with jugs to be filled with warm blood—and are thus accustomed to scenes of violence and cruelty from baby-hood—crime, degeneration, and ferocity are rampant. There is no doubt that butchery debases the community and lowers the tone of public morals. The effect of butchering in blunting moral sensitiveness is shewn by the fact that the number of murders in the United States attributed to butchers exceeds that of any other known avocation; and in many states a slaughterman is not allowed to sit on a jury during a trial for murder."

On the other side, from the point of dietetics flesh-eating is not at all desirable for man. Take the evidence of Sir Benjamin W. Richardson; M.D., F.R.C.S., before the Congress of Public Health. [1] "I sincerely hope that before the close of the (nineteenth) century, not only slaughter-houses will be abolished but that the use of animal flesh as food will be absolutely abandoned." This is not a pious vituperation, but sincere advice given to the world to better its condition by abstaining from meat-eating as it is doubly detrimental to the human body and the nation at large. Montesquieu wrote in connection with meat-eating in India, that it is highly tasteless and insipid in hotter climates especially in countries situated like India in the torrid zone. [2] Mr. Beard

1. *Ibid* p. 19.

2. Quoted in *Hindu Manners, Customs and Ceremonies*, p. 193n.

observes [1] that "vice would certainly decrease, for a bloodless diet promotes the supremacy of the higher self, and poverty would be reduced to a minimum." Again, as Dr. Josiah Oldfield thinks, the slaughter of animals stunts the full growth of the real man. Forcibly Dr. Josiah brings out the truth of the statement in the following words: [2] "Deep down in every human heart there lies the love of fruits and nuts, the longing for the produce of the orchard, and the harvest field and the garden. Deep down in every cultured breast there lies the repulsion against the smells and the sights and the sounds of the shambles of Smithfield. And every human child turns to fruit as instinctively as every feline kitten turns to its prey of flesh and blood.

"What, then, is the future? The past was the diet of *necessity*, the future will be the diet of *selection*. In the first stage man ate what they *could*, in the next stage they ate what they *liked*, and in the last stage they will eat what is *best*, and they will rely upon the ingrained instincts and upon practice to make it agreeable as well as beneficial.

"When man rejects flesh-foods and takes his nutriment direct from nature's hand, of well-matured and healthy fruits and grains and nuts and vegetables with the addition of honey and cheese and milk, we shall find a large number of diseases disappearing, hardy stamina increasing, endurance becoming greater and longevity greatly extended. And I believe that side by side with this diminition of agony inflicted upon animals, will

1. Quoted in *the Cow—My Dumb Mother*. p. 24.
2. *Ibid* pp. 20-21.

come a greater restfulness of mind and body, and a greater freedom from pains and aches, and weariness of flesh, to the human race as a whole."

According to the *Bhagavatgita* man's food consists of *Satva*, *Rajasa* and *Tamasa* which develope respectively the three different orders of human beings in the depreciating order of the superlative. Thus the *Satva* food is the best and consists of articles like fruit and vegetables of the forest. *Rajasa* consists of those forms of food which are due to taste, such as excess of acidity, sourness and pungence. *Tamasa* food consists of animal food and other foods befitting the *Rakshasas*. This line of argument in the *Bhagavatgita* is not simple religious theorising. On the other hand, it contains the crystallised truths of dietetics and the psychological effect of the nature of food taken upon the build of man's sensory organism.

We have now to take into consideration the question of slaughter of animals. Whatever may be the nature of slaughters taking place in regular homes, they deal with domestic pets and, in certain cases, with goats and sheep, while their quantity is not appreciable when compared with the felling of animals in slaughter houses. Even in the houses the best means of putting the victim to a speedy death must be resorted to.

There are two kinds of slaughter houses, public and private. Public slaughter houses consist of those licenced and managed by Municipalities and other local bodies such as District and Taluk Boards. Private slaughter houses are managed by individuals at their own houses and on their own account. The public slaughter houses are governed by the bye-laws of the local bodies which deal with the methods of sanitation and animal hygiene. Whereas the rigour of official supervision in this respect is not appreciable in the case of private slaughter houses.

Government generally frames rules in regard to the general management of the slaughter houses. As illustrations take the two notifications of the Central Provinces and the Madras Provincial Governments. No. 1236—955—XIII of the Central Provinces Government of 31st May 1922 in exercise of the powers conferred by section 10 of the Central Provinces Slaughter of Animals Act (Act IV of 1915), which may be taken as the model for other provinces, and No. 679 of the Madras Government (G. O. No. 1481. L & M) of May 1, 1925 deal exhaustively with the construction and conduction of slaughter houses. But the provisions seem to be quite inadequate and they do not deal with the problem of cruelty to animals while they are being slaughtered. Even though art. 7 of Section 42 of the Madras Act provides that "every person employed in the slaughtering of animals shall use such instruments and appliances and shall adopt such methods of slaughtering and otherwise take such precautions as may be requisite to secure the infliction of as little pain or suffering as practicable," [1] it has not got the surety of practically being applied to mitigate the suffering of animals before they are slaughtered. Governmental legislation must be more drastic.

1. *Fort St. George Gazette*. June 23.1925. No. 25. p. 288.

I will now proceed to give an exposition of the horrors suffered by animals by quoting two graphic accounts by two writers, one from Russia and the other from our own country. Count Leo Tolstoi gave vent to his sincere emotions when he saw a ghastly series of incidents in an abbattoir. The hearts of all readers of his pen-picture will be pricked and they will surely search their hearts whether there is any vestige of the humanitarian element to be found therein. He speaks: [1]

"It was the Friday before Trinity. It was a warm June day . . . . The 'work' was in full swing. All the dusty yard was full, and cattle had been driven into all the little yards beside the 'chambers'.

"At the gate stood carts with oxen, cows and calves tied to them. Other carts drawn by fine horses holding live calves with their heads hanging dangling down, were unloaded, and other carts containing the carcasses of oxen, with shaking legs and heads protruding, and bright-red lungs and crimson livers, were driving *away* from the slaughter-house.

"Through the door opposite to that where I stood, a big red well-fed ox was being led in. Two men were pulling him. He had hardly been led in, when I saw a butcher raise a knife upon his neck, and stab. The ox, as if all its four legs had suddenly been broken, fell heavily upon its belly, then turned over and began to struggle with its legs and hind part.

"Immediately another butcher threw himself upon the front part of the ox, on the side opposite from the

1. Quoted in *the Cow—My Dumb Mother*. pp. 15-19.

struggling legs, caught its horns, and twisted its head down upon the ground, while another butcher cut its throat with a knife, and from under the head poured forth a stream of dark-red blood, under which a blood-besmeared boy placed a tin basin.

"While all this was being done the ox twitched its head incessantly, as if endeavouring to get up, and fought with its legs in the air. The basin was soon full, but the ox was still alive, heaving with heavy gasps and kicking out all four legs, so that the butchers held aloof.

"When one basin was full, the boy carried it away on his head to the Albumin Factory and another boy placed another basin, and this one was also filled. But the ox still heaved his body and struggled with his hind legs.

"When the blood ceased to flow the butcher raised the ox's head and began to skin it. (The ox still writhed.) The head skinned, showed red with white veins, and stayed in positions as the butcher moved it; from both sides of it the skin hung down. The ox did not cease writhing.

"Then another butcher caught the animal by the leg and broke it, and cut it off. In the stomach and other legs the convulsions still went on. The other legs were cut off and thrown. Then the carcass was dragged away and hung up; and *then* the convulsions ceased. The convulsions were over at last.

"Thus from the door I watched the second, third, fourth ox. It was the same with all. The head cut off with the tongue bitten, the same convulsions. The only difference was that the butcher did not always hit his blow so as to fell the ox. Sometimes the butcher missed his aim, then the ox leapt up, roared and covered with blood, tried to escape. But then he was pulled under the bar, hit a second time and felled.

"I afterwards went round to the door through which the oxen entered. Here I saw the same, only nearer and more clearly; and moreover, I here saw what I had missed seeing from the other door, how the oxen were forced to enter. Each time that the ox was taken in the yard and pulled forward by a rope tied to its horns, the ox smelling blood, refused to enter, sometimes roared and retreated backwards. Two men could not drag it by force, and therefore each time one of the butchers went round behind, grasped the ox's tail and twisted it, breaking the stump so that the gristle cracked, and the ox advanced.

"When they had finished the oxen of one owner, they led in another's cattle. Of this next lot, the first animal was not an ox, but a bull. A well-bred, fine, muscular, energetic young animal, black, with white spots and legs. He was pulled: he lowered his head and sternly resisted. But the butcher following behind, caught at his tail, just like an engineman grasping the handle of the whistle, twisted, and the gristles crackled. The bull rushed forward, knocking down the men who were pulling the ropes; then again stopped, squinting with its black eyes, the whites of which were suffused with blood.

"Again the tail crackled, and the bull jumped forward, and was in the spot where they desired him to be.

The striking man approached, took aim, and hit. The hit missed the mark. The bull leaped, shook its head, roared and covered with blood, got free and rushed out. All the men in the doorway jumped aside. But the ready butchers, with the pluck bred by perpetual risks, quickly caught the rope, the tail operation was repeated, and again the bull was in the chamber, where he was dragged under the bar from which he could not escape. The striking man quickly took aim at the spot where the hair separates like a star, and which he found, despite the blood, and then the fine animal, full of life, fell down and writhed its limbs while it was being bled, and its head was cut off.

" 'There the cursed devil has even fallen on the wrong side', gumbled the butcher, cutting the vein upon its head.

"In five minutes they stuck up a head, red instead of black, without skin, with fixed and glassy eyes which had shown with such glorious colours only five minutes before."

Again, take the recent observations of Mr. M. Singaravelu, one of the Municipal Councillors of the Madras Corporation. In a surprise visit paid by him to the Corporation Slaughter-House he is quite shocked at the scene enacted before him, and he writes: [1] "It was yesterday evening that I was informed in the Councillor's room, that some members of the Health Committee paid a visit to the Municipal Slaughter-House at Pulianthope, and witnessed a grue-some spectacle of sheep being

---

1. *Corporation Slaughter Houses*: A letter sent by Mr. M. Singaravelu to the *Justice*, Madras dated 6-2-'26.

slaughtered one over the other, while they were undergoing death spasms in the immediate presence of live sheep. ....On entering the slaughter house this morning, I was shocked to see batches of five sheep were kept standing in close proximity to the dying ones, and cut in succession, while all the cut ones were struggling in death spasms. This horrible act went on till the whole batch was despatched and left writhing in death's agony. It was dreadful to look at the poor things bleating as they were dragged to death, and the sight seemed more dreadful than the sight pictured to us by Upton Sinclair in his "Jungles" which shocked the whole world a few years ago. But the amazing thing is that ample provision is made in the slaughter house itself, for killing the sheep away from the living ones, and thereby prevent this monstrous cruelty, and yet this cruelty is allowed to be perpetrated in the very presence two Corporation Superintendents. So far, no satisfactory explanation was forthcoming for the perpetration of this disgusting cruelty upon these dumb creatures in the immediate presence of their dying fellows undergoing death's tortures. *Only an irresponsible Corporation, irresponsible for the sanctity of life, both of man and of beast can tolerate so long such an act of cruelty. Indifference to suffering is cruel enough, but to see it perpetrated or condoned by a Corporation is shocking.*

The remedy for this debased method of butchery surely lies in the inculcation of the principle of humanitarianism and a popularisation of the emotion of mercy, besides stringent legislation on the part of the authorities under whose supervision these slaughter-houses are conducted. Propaganda in this respect is sure to succeed

Another method lies in the process of guillotining the animal and the instruments used in severing off the necks of the animals from their bodies. Experts in the line have struggled hard in improvising means towards minimising the pain given to animals while they are slaughtered. "An Expert" writing in the *Sunday Times* of Lahore on the "Humane Killer—Should it be adopted", reviews the present impeachable processes of slaughtering animals and brings out the efficiency of this instrument in abolishing "a vast amount both of cruelty and unintentional suffering inseperable from the old methods." As this piece of perishable journalism is not available to all, I insert below an excerpt from that article, for the information of my readers : "The compulsory use of a humane killer in animals slaughtered for food is long overdue. There can be no doubt that its adoption would abolish a vast amount both of cruelty and unintentional infliction of suffering inseperable from the old methods. The repeated blows which animals often receive from tho pole aze, the flat hammer, and other implements, before being rendered unconscious, could not occur with the humane killer. In order to allay any possible doubt in the minds of any of my readers, let me say that I possess abundant evidence on this matter. Only recently, in Bombay, I myself saw a poor animal receive a pole-axe puncture near the eye, after which it was thrashed with the flat axe in order to get it back into position for another blow. At Calcutta and other places, I have examined heads with many punctures and also witnessed more suffering than my readers could bear to hear described. Not once but many times have butchers said to me ; How can anyone in our trade deny that these things happen? And yet official representatives of our trade deny it. Only those whose position enables them to be in constant attendance in a slaughter house know of all that takes place there. I have seen an animal, which had given some trouble, being attacked with a cropping knife, and another, whose head was swollen with repeated blows, have the skin cut away from its forehead to allow the pole axe to puncture more easily.

"None of the objections raised against the use of the humane killer will hold good. I have demonstrated with these instruments in Northumberland, Durham, Cumberland, and Scotland for 20 years and never yet met a man who could find fault with the free bleeding of the animals and, though I have invited criticism, I have not found anyone who could point out to me faulty setting, or challenge the keeping quality of the meat. Carlisle has given a reply to these questions, which has never been disproved. For nearly a quarter of a century the use of the humane killer has been compulsory on cattle in that city. During that time seven representatives of the meat trade have been on the City Council. To-day one butcher is an alderman. In a letter before me he says: 'I highly recommend the humane killer for safety and quickness. I get the animal bled more easily, the blood flows freer, owing to the neck not being crooked. As to the keeping quality of the meat, I find no difference, except that in some cases it keeps better, owing to the cattle having been quiet and not excited as I have seen them with the pole axe I would not go back to the pole axe or hammer again.'

"The point I want to deal with at some length is whether or not blood spots or "splashing" in pork is the result of the shooting of pigs. Does the heart's action cease immediately after a pig has been shot? The vigorous reflex action and the manner in which the bleeding occurs demonstrate to the trained observer that both the heart and lungs are still in action. There is no reason why the bleeding should be impeded. Close personal observation and long experience enable me to state definitely that "Splashing" occurs in swine quite independently of the method of slaughtering, and has nothing whatsoever to do with it. I have frequently seen it in cattle, and remember one very fine heifer, the meat of which was so badly splashed as to be unsaleable. In this animal there were no outward signs indicating the state the flesh was found in when cut up. That animal was slaughtered with the pole axe. I have before me now one of the finest specimens of splashed pork I have ever seen, which has been sent to me for inspection; and this pork is from an unshot pig.

"I have asked a slaughterer engaged in a firm of bacon curing and his answer is precisely the same, that the meat is perfectly clean.

"I obtained permission from a very large frim of pork butchers to shoot a sow with the humane killer and to compare it with one that had been pole-axed. The shot pig was beautiful and white, and well set, while in the other one, many of the veins were not drained of blood. I hold a report from the owner endorsing my report on the shot pig and stating that no fault could be found with the carcase. Another man who, like the pork butcher just mentioned, does not use the humane killer, asked me to shoot three large pigs, about 280 pounds each, as their heads were so hard that he usually had a difficulty in getting the other instrument in. He now informs me that the pigs are cut up and are in excellent condition, the meat being white with no spots splashing."

To conclude, man must be capable of using to profit, and general beneficience the instinct of humanitarianism in all his dealings with the animal kingdom. If total obstinence from taking animal life is not possible, at least clemency and quicker methods of despatching the brutes causing them the least possible pain must be resorted to.

CHAPTER IX.

MEDICINAL VALUES OF THE PRODUCTS OF THE COW

"THE Materia Medica of the Hindus is a marvel to the modern investigator. In it are fully described the properties of drugs belonging to the animal, vegetable, and mineral kingdoms, and the articles of food essential to the maintance of health and strength." Thus writes the Thakore Saheb of Gondol in his *Short History of the Aryan Medical Science.*[1] Our Aryan ancestors were famous in every branch of human knowledge, and in respect of the medical science, their stock of knowledge, intuitive powers of investigation, and indefatigable researches left no stone unturned. Marvellous as is their *materia medica*, we find ourselves amazed when we realise that modern developments of allopathic medicine, clinical science and medical chemistry prove to us the wonderful advance made by our ancestors in the field of diognosis of the properties of substances and the careful application of the results of their investigations in curing human ailments.

We brand the medical practices of our ancestors as crude, and deride them. Thus, when we find that cow-dung is advised as a poutice we discard it as a barbarous practice. But western medical science is contributing its quota in proving to the world the sanity of

1 *A Short History of the Aryan Medical Science*: By H. H. Sir Bhagavat Sinh Jee. K.C.I.E., M.D., D.C.L., L. L. D., F.R.S.E., London, Macmillan & Co., 1896. p. 101.

this kind of medical treatment as propounded by our ancestors.

In this chapter, I will limit my investigations to the properties of the products of the cow. Cow's milk, urine and dung are taken one by one and their place in Aryan medical science is ascertained first. Then the latest clinical researches are incorporated *in extenso* to prove the rationale of these Aryan practices. The problem of vaccination and its toll upon cow-life is, for the sake of convenience, treated here.

The excellent qualities of cow's milk are so obvious on the surface that no recommendation of their use in cases of debility and convalescence seems to be necessary. The superiority of cow's milk over even human milk is pronounced. Take the average composition of human milk : [1].

Proteids	2·00
Fat	3·55
Sugar milk	6·20
Salts	2·50
Water	85·75

In contrast to this take the average composition of cow's milk :

Proteids (casein etc)	4·00
Fat (butter)	3·90
Lactose (sugar of milk)	4·02
Salts	0·73
Water	86·20
Specific gravity	0·30

1 These tables are taken from *Hygiene and Diseases of India*, By Lieut. Col. Patrick Hehir. I.M.S., Madras, Higginbothams Ltd., Third Edition, p. 189.

It will be plain that milk may be as freely used as water provided it is available in the desirable quantity. In modern India, especially, when low vitality and heavy mortality reign supreme, the value of milk can in no way be exaggerated. Such are the excellent nourishment-producing qualities of milk that it is regarded as a purificatory agency. "Cow's are auspicious purifiers, upon cows depend the four worlds."[1] According to Aryan tradition, one of the first things which a person ought to do on rising is to look at curds and ghee if he desires a long life.[2] The Thakore Saheb of Gondol thus sums up the value of milk in Aryan medicine :[3] "*Dugdha* (milk) is nutritive and vitalising. . . . . . Cow's milk increases the secretion of semen . . . The properties of milk are said to vary according to the colour of the animal and the qualities of pasture. The chief preparations of milk are *Dadhi* (curds), a favourite remedy for diarrhoea ; *Takar* (whey), which is refrigerant ; *Navanita* (butter) used in constipation ; *Ghrita* (clarified butter), is tonic, emollieunt and cooling : *Santanika* (cream), is strong thening."

According to Aryan surgery, wounds must be dressed at regular intervals. Should the wound cause intense pain, the application of a cloth drenched in tepid *ghee* is efficacious in palliating the pain and effecting a speedy cure.[4] So much for milk and its collateral products and their values in Aryan medicine.

---

1 *Institutes of Vishnu.* xxiii. 57. Translated by Dr. Julius Jolly. S.S.E. Vol. VII. p. 105.

2 *A Short History of Aryan Medical Science.* p. 59.

3 *Ibid* p. 130.

4 *Ibid.* p. 182.

Abbé Dubois writes that "to purify the body from any interior defilement that it may have been contracted, there is no more efficacious way than by the performance of the panchagaviya"[1] While speaking of the Zorastrian attitude, we have seen how Ahura Mazda advices Zarathustra about the process of ablutions to be undergone in order to purify any defiled human being.[2] In fact, the Indo-Iranian civilizations always attach special significance to urine. Our sacred texts always make urine play an important part in ablutions. Thus, the urine of the cow is one of "those six excellent productions of the cow which are always propitious."[3] "In the urine of the cow dwells the Ganges."[4] The reason for this wide-spread use of urine is not far to seek. "*Muthra* (urine) would appear to be a very useful agent according to the Hindoos, and has a very wide application. Cow's urine is used both internally and externally. It is prescribed in colic and other diseases."[5] Cow's urine is used extensively in purifying metals. In purifying tin cow's urine is an useful solvent.[6] In the purging of "the impurities of ores, whether superficial or inseparably combined with them," cow's bile and urine are invaluable.[7] "Permanent softness (mrdu stambha) is also

1. *Hindu Manners, Customs and Ceremonies.* p. 106. Cf. *Omens and Superstitions of Southern India* by Edgar Thurston. C.I.E., London, T. Fisher Unwin. 1912. p 79.

2. *Zend-Avesta. Fargard.* vii. 56-65. S. B. E., Vol. IV. pp. 91-2.

3. *Institutes of Vishnu.* xxiii. 58-9. S. B. E. Vol. VII. p. 105.

4. *Ibid.* verse 61. *Ibid.*

5. *A Short History of Aryan Medical Science.* pp. 132-3.

6. *Ibid* p. 140.

7. Kautilya's *Arthasastra*, Trans. by Dr. R. Shama Sastri. 2nd. Edition. 1923. p. 93.

attained when the metal is treated with the powder of cow's teeth and horn."[1] Kautilya mentions the various uses to which cow dung and urine can be put in the purification of metals.[2] We are not justified in regarding all these practices as crude and utterly visionary, if we are to remember the modern methods of medicine and metullurgy. Modern science is unfolding to us the merits of these practices of our ancestors.

Likewise is the case of cow-dung. John Lockwood Kipling says:[3] "The rustic pharmacy of most countries knows the value of the substance as a poultice, but in India the sanctity of the cow lends a semi-sacred sanction to its use, and its application has the prestige as well as the mechanical attraction of a cataplasm." This statement is fully justified in the light of our *Dharmasastras*. According to the *Institutes of Vishnu*:[4] "A house is purified by scouring it with a broom and plastering the ground with cow-dung, and a manuscript or book by sprinkling water over it. Land is cleansed by plastering with cow-dung." In Aryan medical science, cow-dung plays an important part. "*Purisha* (dung) of a cow is applied to parts of the skin that may be inflamed or discoloured. It is occasionally given inside. In India it is used for plastering the walls, and is spread on floors under the impression that it possesses disinfecting

---

1. *Ibid.*
2. *Ibid.* Bk. II. Chs. xii and xii.
3. *Beast and Man India.* A popular treatise of Indian animals and their relations with the people. By John Lockwood Kipling C. I. E., Macmillan & Co., 1892. Second Edn. p. 149.
4. xxiii. 56. S. B. E. Vol. VII. p. 105.

qualities."[1] Cow-dung is extensively used in India. As a poultice it is most famous and efficacious. "Cow-dung ashes are *blanche pearle* and the raw substance is the ordained cosmetic of the Hindu devotees."[2]

Cow-dung is used invariably in plastering the walls and floors of an Indian home. This is universal in the rural parts of India, even though, in the urban areas, owing to the impact of western civilization and higher ideas of decency, it is generally abandoned in favour of white-washing. It is an effective agent as a bactericide and prevents infection, as we shall presently see in the light of western clinical research. Says Lockwood Kipling:[3] "As a cement, cow-dung takes a high place as the finishing coat of the floor and the mud-wall. This coating is renewed at frequent intervals, and periodically applied to earthern floors. During the process of smearing the odour is somewhat strong, but this passes away in an incredibly short time, leaving an undeniable impression of coolness, freshness and, strange it may seem, fragrance." This opinion is endorsed by another weighty authority from the west who says:[4] "Indian houses are kept beautifully clean. Floors and walls are plastered from time to time by the women with a mixture of cow-dung and mud, which for the purpose is much more efficient than it would appear." We need not comment upon this unqualified testimony of pronounced authorities and we have to only regret that our

1. *A Short History of Aryan Medical Science* p. 134.
2. *Beast and Man in India.* p. 150.
3. *Ibid.*
4. *Studies in Indian Life and Sentiment.* By Sir Bampfylde Fuller. K. C. S. I., C. I. E., London, John Murray 1910. p. 151.

cantemporaries in the west are required to show us the proper paths of appreciation of our hoary practices.

We will now pass on to the results of the investigations of western scientists which justify in a full measure the sanity of our ancient forefathers in emphasising the importance of urine and cow-dung for internal as well as external application. Professors Symmers of Belfast and Kirk of Ulster conducted a series of experiments twelve years back upon the clinical values of urea, and crystallised their investigations to the amazement of the western medical world and to the gratification of us, sons of the Aryan line, to whom those results were long familiar, but requiring ampler exposition from a scientific point of view. They conclude their investigations with seven principles underlying the utility of urea : [1]

"1. From our laboratory and clinical tests we conclude that urea as antiseptic acts in the presence of blood.

2. That it is innocuous to animal tissues.

3. That in the quantities that can be used in wounds it is non-toxic.

4. That by its use at least half the labour necessitated by other methods of treatment is saved.

1. *The Lancet*. 4th December 1915. Article on "Urea as a Bactericide and its application in the treatment of wounds." By W. St. C. Symmers, Prof: of pathology, Queen's University, Belfast; and T. S. Kirk, Principal Medical Officer, Ulster Volunteer Force.

I am highly obliged to my friend Mr. K. V. Subba Rao of the Madras Medical College, for having traced this back number for my sake from the archieves of the Connemara Library, and copying the article specially to facilitate my investigations. My thanks are due to him for the services done in this respect.

5. That during its use, the processes of repair are not at all retarded.

6. We believe that the most striking results will be obtained by its use as a first-aid dressing.

7. It prevents suppuration arising in wounds from chronic blood infections."

Prof: Symmers during the course of the article observes: "Thus in urea we have a substance which in the dry state is pronouncedly stable, which is practically non-poisonous, and which even in low concentration (3 per cent) affects the growth of bacteria, ... and which is markedly bactericidal to nonsporing bacteria in the higher percentages. This bactericidal effect is active in the presence of blood and such like organic fluids."

Another set of experiments performed by Drs. Crawford, Hamilton and McIntosh of America has proved quite recently the use of urea as a diuretic in advanced heart failure. Before summing up their investigations, it is only proper for me to mention the practice enjoined by our ancestors of making an extensive use of *Panchagavya* which certains milk, urine, dung, sour-milk, butter and *Gorochana* (a pigment prepared out of the bile and urine of a cow). In the course of their experiments the learned doctors say:[1] "Urea was given with a view to re-establishing a normal water-balance by maintaining an adequate urine output, and also when slight oedema has collected to bring about its removal." The following

1. Quoted in *The Antiseptic*. Edited by the Hon'ble U. Rama Rao and U. Krishna Rao, Madras. March 1926. Vol. XXIII. No. 3. pp. 168-169.

passage brings out the unfailing efficacy of urea in advanced cases of heart failure. "As soon as the administration of urea was stopped, the urinary output immediately fell and the clinical condition became worse. When treatment was resumed an improvement again took place. The increase in urine output varied with the dose and followed closely by the curve of urea excretion. With continuous administration the daily volume was maintained at an almost constant level." The article concludes, "by suggesting that urea is a useful drug in cases of heart-failure with oedema in which the treatment of the cardiac condition has failed to remove the oedema or maintain an adequate water excretion."

I have now only to treat of vaccination and conclude this chapter. The Sardar Saheb of Gondol writes: [1] "Inoculation for small-pox seems to have been known from a very early age. Long before Edward Jenner was born, certain classes in India, especially cow-herds, shepherds, chamars and the like had been in the habit of collecting and preserving the dry scabs of pustules. A little of this they used to place on the forearm, and puncture the skin with a needle. In consequence of this inoculation the classes are supposed to have enjoyed a certain amount of immunity from small-pox. Dr. Huillet, late of Pondichery, assures us that 'Vaccination was known to a physician, Dhanvantri, who flourished before Hippocratus.' In preparing the lymph used in inoculation in case of small-pox, a toll is levied on the cow-life in India. My friend Dr. K. Doraiswami Naidu, the local veterinary officer at Masulipatam, informs me that

1. *A Short History of Aryan Medical Science*, p. 179.

the cows selected for the purpose of extracting the lymph do not thrive well after the process of operation is undergone. The outer portion of the abdomen of the selected cow-calf is first of all shaven, and the small-pox bacilli injected into its system. The pustules develop on the prepared portion of the belly and from them lymph is extracted. After this it is confined to refrigerent rooms. It is then packed, after a process of purification, into tin tubes and is thus made available for public use. This cumbrous process, while causing pain both to the animal and to us who will have to get inoculated by means of punctures on the fore-arm, is involving an appreciable toll upon cow life in India.

But, thanks to Prof: Besredka of the Pasteur Institute, Paris, this toll upon cow-life is taken away at the present day. He conclusively proved that immunity is a local thing in the case of small-pox. Inoculation by puncturing the fore-arm is quite unnecessary and the circulating system as a whole need not be disturbed. The usual process of obtaining lymph may well be abandoned. "The new method of Prof: Besredka suffers from none of the disadvantages, since the immunising agent contained in tabloid form, is taken through the mouth, has no untoward reactions, and is perfectly safe for infants, invalids and the aged. At present the injection of dead culture into the blood-stream is intended to induce a general immunity, but the Besredka theory is this: that as all invading micro-organisms have a selective affinity for some particular organ, so there should be a definite protective vaccine for each organ. Thus he found out that dysentery and cholera bacilli make their way straight to the intestinal wall; a rabbit was inoculated with these bacilli through a vein in its ear, and was killed five hours later. The autopsy showed all the bacilli on the intestinal wall—they had made their way there as fast as they could, disdaining all other homes. All that is necessary then to immunise against dysentary or cholera is to immunise the intestinal wall, since this is the only organ open to attack and the best way of immunising it is by the most direct route, that is through the mouth. But there was difficulty in the way for the dead bacilli in the tablet could not find their way through the wall at all times. Only and when there was a free execretion of bile was ingress possible. Prof: Besredka's solution to this difficulty was to include in the tabloid a certain portion of synthesised bile to act as a sort of key to the gates on the wall of the intestine." [1]

This is only a recent discovery and has just made its way into India. Modest quantities of Prof: Bcsredka's tabloids are now being used. A popularising of this harmless kind of treatment would remove the strain put upon the life of the cow as entailed by the ordinary methods of obtaining vaccine, and thus prove to be an asset to India as far as the cattle of the country are concerned.

1. *Kalpaka: The Psychic Review of the East.* Article on "Vaccination through the mouth". April 26, 1926. Vol. XXI. No. 4, p. 159-60.

CHAPTER X.

HISTORY OF COW-PROTECTION IN INDIA.

" IMMEMORIAL custom is trancendent law, approved in the sacred scriptures and in the codes of divine legislation ; let every man, therefore, of the three principal classes who has a due reverence for the supreme spirit which dwells in him, diligently and constantly observe immemorial custom."[1] This dictum of Manu may be taken to be the motto for the present chapter. The history of cow-protection in India is one of the brilliant phases of our national strivings which we perpetuate to the end of the world. The cow occupied a prominent place in the out-look of the sons of Bharatavarsha ever since the Aryans set their foot on the Indian soil. Not merely the Aryans of India, but the members of the Aryan stock who will be found dispersed in foreign lands, especially the Indo-Iranians have an exemplary veneration towards bovine cattle. Dr. Macdonnel admirably sums up the influence of the cow upon Indian life and thought, thus :[2] "To no other animal has mankind owed so much, and the debt richly repaid with a veneration unknown in other lands. So important a factor has the cow proved in Indian life and thought that an exhaustive account of her influence from the earliest times of the world would form a noteworthy chapter in the history of civilization."

---

1. *Laws of Manu,* Ch. I. verse. 108.
2. *A History of Sanscrit Literature,* p. 110. (1905).

Such being the importance of the cow to us Indians, it is but obvious that the history of cow-protection in India must have had a very glorious aspect, and we will not feel disappointed when we review the progress of the movement in favour of cow-protection in India.

We cannot afford to ignore the disturbing elements that obstruct the fair progress of the universal movement towards conserving cow life in India. We have already seen that at one time cows and bulls were thought to be fit animals to be slaughtered in sacrifice and several instances are available for us to show that they were actually slaughtered and slaughtered in abundance. We have seen again that the Muhammadan conqueror-settlers of India have a positive hatred towards the Hindu veneration of the cow, and the economic harm their masses have done to the country in taking a toll upon cattle life, especially the bovine cattle whose fundamental importance to Indian agriculture can in no way be minimised. There are other dangers to cattle life in India which mean a loss to national interests. Pestilence, disease, and draughts take a regular toll upon cattle life in India. Besides these there are other dangers of a far more serious kind. Take this significant passage from the pen of a distinguished judge of the East India Company describing the situation of India towards the closing part of the eighteenth and the early decades of the nineteenth century. [1] "The Gochores, or cow-stealers, are among the cleverest of deliquents.

1. *Considerations on the Present Political State in India.* Vol. I. p. 129. By Alexandar Fraser Tytler. Assistant Judge of the XXIV Purganas. London. 1815. 2 Vols. A rare set of interesting volumes.

They are chiefly Musalmans and *Motchees*, sometimes joined and often encouraged by the Gowalas. This crime is particularly common in the neighbourhood of Calcutta, and all great towns, where there is a demand for cow's flesh. The intermediate sales are conducted with such rapidity and skill; the animals are so defaced by mutilating their horns and ears, and by the additional marks placed on them, as well as by the loss of flesh, and there are so many different individuals employed in the sale, that the proofs of this become so tedious and frequently impossible." Besides this, there is the annual toll in the shape of cattle poisoning. "There is a class of English Medical Officers known as Chemical Examiners to Government, whose researches have largely contributed to the detection and conviction of cattle poisoners who for centuries have taken a heavy toll on the beast life of the land." [1] "These are not exceptional practices, for in one prison at one time fifteen hundred leather-dressers have been confined for cattle poisoning." [2]

The aggregate harm from all these sources to Indian cattle life can never be of any negligible magnitude. But with all this serious handicap there is a universal craving in India for the conserving of cow life. Efforts were made with never-flagging interest, Indian history is an unqualified testimony to this phase of our national endeavour. With all the bigotry of Indian Muslim rulers, the more liberal among them who form a majority, have not only abstained from killing cows but have

1. *Beast and Man in India.* p. 109.
2. *Ibid* p. 108.

promulgated positive ordinances in the cause of cow-protection.

When we sketch the history of cow-protection in India, for that matter, of any movement in the world, we have to take into consideration the impressionistic effects of pageants and the inspiring grandeur of sights besides the spirit of the exhibitions. Weak points must not be put to any searching scrutiny, while from the numerical point of view these instances must not prejudice the effect of those pageants upon us. We have to gauge the broad general effects, and thus rest satisfied in having obtained a rapid survey of the memorable phases of the history of cow-protection in India.

The efforts at cow-protection that were made successively throughout the general trend of Indian history may, for the sake of convenience and clarity, be divided into two divisions, social and regal. By social legislation I mean the sum total of the efforts of society,—its prejudices, conventions and customs that will produce at times more beneficial and striking results than all the strivings of the rulers of a country. By regal legislation is to be understood the action of the state in the matter, in the shape of public ordinances, prohibitory promulgations, and, later on, at the present day, the embodiments of statutory legislation. In both these respects, the history of cow protection in India has a unique story to recount. We will now take up one by one the two kinds of legislation and trace their history, incorporating in our investigations for the first time the scattered remnants of social and regal effort as they come down to us from contemporary documents, which will enhance the clear impressiveness of our pageant.

The attitude of the Hindu religious lore and the general trend of Hindu traditional beliefs towards cow-life are the effective instruments in preparing the way for the movement of genuine cow protection. In a primitive age, Aryan India might have considered bovine cattle as fit offerings for sacrifice. But the more salutory phases of Indian outlook generally preserved in tact the strivings of the generality of the Hindu population, in protecting cow life.

The cow has always inspired a certain amount of reverential awe in the mind of the ancient Aryans. As such it is but natural for us to expect in their sacred codifications injunctions of an imperative kind that go a long way in directing social action in respect of its relation to cow-life. The fundamental importance of bovine cattle to the Indian agriculture of the Aryan times had had its effects upon the codifiers of our sacred texts who freely indulged in hyperboles and commedatory metaphors while describing the sanctity of cow-life. In the light of the Hindu theories so far worked out in an earlier chapter, it will be apparent that the cow is regarded by our ancestors as the central point in creation and signifies the sustaining stamina of the word. I need not go here into details as regards the position of the cow in Indian sentiment, as it has been fully exposed elsewhere. Suffice it to say that the cow is an earthly deity even more exalted at times than the Brahmans.

The Buddhist creed following in the wake of decadant Hinduism has contributed, along with its famous harbinger Jainism, not an insignificant quota towards sanctifying life on earth,—animal life included. We have found that Buddha applied an effective break to the trend of the Brahmanical type of sacrifice. We have found that the Order consisted of Bhikkus who led exemplary lives of humaneness. We have found that animal hospitals were established throughout the length and breath of the country. We have seen how animal slaughter had been stopped in the royal kitchens of Asoka and Harsha Vardhana. Thus the *dharma* of the Buddhist creed emphasised all the more the sacredness of cattle life and in particular cow life to the world.

The general legacy of Aryan civilization has been so scrupulously preserved in all the ages through which India has passed, that even at the present day we show the same tenacity in preserving cow life. I will now cite a few passages from contemporary travellers and inhabitants of India to prove that at no stage of Indian history has the generality of the population showed any signs of slackness in their endeavours to preserve cow-life from extinction or abuse.

Marco Polo, the Venetion traveller who was the first man to give us an account of the XIII century conditions of the East, emphasises the veneration of the Hindu towards the ox in those days of excessive national ordeal and dishonour under the severe yoke of the aggressive Muhammadans who were notorious for their hatred of the Hindu beliefs in the sanctity of cow-life.[1] "The greater part of the idolatrous inhabitants of

1 *The Travels of Marco Polo the Venetian*. p. 357. Everyman's Library. 1914. with an introduction by John Masefield.

this kingdom show particular reverence to the ox; none will from any consideration be induced to eat the flesh of oxen. But there is a particular class of men termed gaui, who although many of them eat of the flesh, yet they dare not kill the animal; but when they find a carcase whether it had died a natural death or otherwise, the gaui eat it; and all descriptions of people daub their houses with cow-dung." Buchanan writing in his Journal about his journey through the Carnatic, expresses the same observations.[1] "The people of this part of the country consider the ox as a living God, who gives them their bread; and in every village there are one or two bulls, to whom weakly or monthly worship is performed . . . . . . On the north of the Cauvery this superstition is not prevalent. The bull is there considered as respectable on account of Iswara having chosen one of them for his steed." Marco Polo observe again:[2] "Those amongst them who pay adoration to the ox, take with them, when they go to battle, the hair of a wild bull, which they attach to the manes of their horses, believing its virtue and efficiency to be such, that every one who carries it about with him is secure from all kind of danger." Francois Bernier, travelling in India in the XVII century observes the same phenomna even at the Mughal court. According to him,[3] "The *Gentiles* believe in a doctrine similar to that of the *Pythagoreans* with regard to the transmigration of souls,

1 Vol. II, p. 174. Quoted *Ibid* foot-note.

2 *Loc. Cit.* pp. 365-366.

3 *Travels in the Mogul Empire.* pp. 326-327. by Francois Bernier. Translated by Archbald Constable. Second Edition. Revised by V. A. Smith, Oxford (1914).

and hold it illegal to kill or eat animals, an exception being made, however, in favour of a few of the second tribe, provided the flesh is not that of the cow or the peacock. For these two animals they feel a peculiar respect, particularly for the cow, imagining that it is by holding to cow's tail they are to cross the river which separates this life from the next . . . . . or this superior regard for the cow may more probably be owing to her extraordinary usefulness as being the animal which supplies them milk and butter (a considerable part of their aliment), and which may be considered a source of husbandry, consequently the preserver of life itself." Abbe Dubois travelling in India towards the close of the XVIII century writes [1] that "to eat the flesh of a cow is an ineffaceable defilement, The bare idea of tasting it would be abhorrent to any Hindu." According to Tytler, the current notions among the people of Bengal in the early decades of the last century strongly favour the supreme value put upon cow-life. [2] "The life of a cow is of much greater consequence than the life of a Sooder ; and in some parts of the Shasters is reckoned to that of a Brahman."

These passages from testimonies of modern visitors of India have been selected to illustrate the general attitude of the Hindus towards the cow for a cogent reason. By the time these writers visited India, Muhammadan suzeramity over the country was established. "Superorganic evolution" of Herbert Spencer has begun

1 *Hindu Manners Customs and Ceremonies.* p. 193. Translated by H. K. Beauchamp.

2 *Considerations on the Present Political State of India.* Vol. I. p. 263. (1815).

her proselytising influence. The Muhammadans were deliberately trying to treat with contempt the sentiments of the Hindus regarding the cow. Cow slaughter was openly perpetrated to the face of the Hindus. There is the force of the conqueror nation's will behind all these phenomena. Yet during these momentous periods of Indian History, Indians never showed signs of despair or indifference towards protecting cow life. From this, when a retrospective glance is cast upon the ages past when Hindu kingdoms flourished, we must but imagine, and rightly too, that Hindu sentiment must have been quite inveterate as far as any infringement upon cow-life is concerned.

Regal legislation in India towards protecting cow life has a memarable history of its own. Not only Hindu sovereigns, but Muhammadan conquerors of India have striven their best for the cause of cow-protection. Even when compared with the social legislation of Manu wherein he declares cow-killing to be a *Upapathaka*,[1] and the Hindu law according to Vasistha [2] which inflicts a *Taptakrikhkhara* penance npon the perpetrator of cow-slaughter and allied legislation, the attitude and strivings in general of the state in India have a favourable comparison and at times a decided advantage over it. We will now set ourselves towards working out the history of cow-protection in India from this line of investigation tracing regal legislation as far as available from the infancy of Indian civilization.

---

1 *Laws of Manu.* Ch. xi. verse, 60.

2 *Vasistha Dharmasastra.* xxii. 23. S. B. E. Vol. XIV. p. 113.

Indian history abounds in instances which show in clear terms the genuine efforts of the state towards protecting cow life. The very constitution of the Hindu is surcharged with veneration towards the cow. "The genuine Hindu *dharma* exacts from among other things veneration to the Brahmans, respect for the sanctity of animal life in various degrees, and especially veneration for horned cattle, pre-eminently the cow."[1] State action received powerful stimulus from this general legacy of the Aryan *dharma.*

The regular history of India may be said to begin with the invasion of Alexandar.[2] Prior to his ivasion, even though we find several sources for writing a regular history of India, much of our material is of a legendary character losing much of precision and utterly unknown of chronological sequence. Thus while we are offered statements full of exaggeration we find our endeavours generally futile, whatever may be the output of genuine research by the famous Indologists of the world, as far as chronology is concerned. The historical sense may be said to be the legacy of the Muhammadan conquerors of India.[3] In the other respect of social and economic history, we may say that ancient India may be given the first place among all countries, with the exception of Greece, in that she preserved a wealth of material embedded in the

1 *Oxford History of India.* p. 34. By V. A. Smith. Oxford (1920).

2 *Early History of India.* Introduction p. 1. By V. A. Smith. Oxford University Press. Third Edition. 1914.

3. *Mughal Administration.* Readership lectures of the Patna University, by Jadunath Sarkar.

epic lore and other socialogical documents, only wanting to be unearthed by scholars after systematic study.[1] Thus when we consider the history of cow-protection we have only to deal mostly with the sentimental attitude of the ancient Aryans towards the sanctity of the cow. This we have seen in the earlier chapters.

Regular historical evidence regarding state interference in cow-protection is to be found only after Asoka. Buddhist endevour had completely triumphed in proscribing all forms of Brahmanical sacrifice, and the general legacy of *dharma* having for its main-stay the principle of humaneness was established. The task of Asoka was thus made easier. Especially, after his experiences of the Kalinga war, Asoka set himself towards the protection of animal life, even waiving the necessity of the royal kitchen to slaughter animals for doling out food and drink to the needy and the poor. His Rock and Pillar Edicts supply us with our main sources of information. Animal hospitals were established by Buddha thoughout the country. Asoka made for the efficient organisation of such charitable institutions and provided ample facilities for medical treatment of animals. Minor Rock Edict II emphasises that "respect for living creatures should be made firm."[2]

1. The *Vedas*, especially the *Rig* and *Atharvana Vedas*, Manu, Kautilya, Sukra, and other authors supply us with useful mines of information regarding the economic conditions of Ancient India. While the religious beliefs and practices of the Aryans, are to be found in the multitudinous host of *Brahmanas*, *Dharmasastras* and *Puranas*. These have not as yet been completely exhausted to give us a final and comprehensive picture of ancient Indian life.

2. *Asoka*, Carmichael Lectures by D. R. Bhandarkar, M.A., Ph. D., (1923) p. 330. Cf. Rock Edict. III. *Ibid.*, p. 278.

Pillar Edict V is a lasting testimony to the fervent desires of Asoka in the cause of the protection of animal life,—his special legislation towards the prevention of cruelty towards the bulls during the process of castration is noteworthy, and may be quoted in full.[1] "Thus saith king Priyadarsin, Beloved of the gods :—When I had been consecrated twenty-six years, the following animals were declared unworthy of slaughter, namely, parrots, starlings, ruddy geese, swans, *Nandimukhas*, *Gelatas*, flying-foxes, queen-ants, female tortoises, boneless fish, *Vedaveyakas*, *Ganga-Paputakas*, skates, tortoises and porcupines, hare-like squirrels, twelve-antler stags, bulls set free, household vermin, rhinoceros, grey doves, village pigeons, and all quadrupeds which are neither used nor eaten. She goats, ewes, aud sows, which are with young or in milk, are unworthy of slaughter, and some of their young ones up to six months of age. Cocks shall not be caponed. Chaff containing living things shall not be burnt. Forests shall not be set on fire either for mischief or for the destruction of life. The living shall not be fed with the living. About the full moon of each of the three seasons and the full moon of Tishya, fish may neither be killed nor sold during three days, namely the fourteenth (and) the fifteenth (of the fortnight) and the first (of the following fortnight), and certainly not on fast days. On the same days these and other species of life also shall not be killed in the elephant forest and fish preserves. On the eighth of (each) fortnight and on the fourteenth and fifteenth, on the Tishya and Punarvasu days, on the full-moon days of the three seasons,—on (such) auspicious days, bulls

1. *Ibid.*, pp. 314-15.

shall not be castrated: he-goats, rams, boars and such others as are castrated shall not be castrated. On the Tishya and Punarvasu days, on the full-moon days of the seasons, and during the fortnights connected with the full-moons of the seasons, the branding of horses and oxen shall not be done. Twenty-five jail deliveries have been effected by me, who am consecrated twenty-six years just in that period." Rock Edict II [1] points to the establishment of *Pinjrapoles* which will be dealt with in greater detail subsequently, and repeats that "King Priyadarsin, Beloved of the gods, established medical treatment of two kinds,—that wholesome for men and that wholesome for animals." Kautilya describing the politico-economic conditions of Ancient India emphasises the importance of the state regulation of cattle life and meeting their necessities. Special Superintendents of Cows were to be appointed.[2] "He should superintend herds maintained for wages; herds surrendered for a fixed amount of dairy produce; useless and abandoned herds; herds maintained by a share in dairy produce;[3] classes of herds; cattle that strayed; cattle that are irrecoverably lost; and the amassed quantity of milk and clarified butter." This is in perfect accordance with the Aryan Science of *Varta* generally addressed to be the fit occupation of the Vaisyas. "In *Varta* are treated interest, agriculture, commerce and preservation of cows."[4] With the progress of civic action and definite

1. *Ibid*, p. 276.
2. Bk. II. Ch. xxxix. Shamsastri, 2nd Edn. pp. 155-159.
3. Cf. *Laws of Manu*, viii. 231.
4. *Sukranitt.* I. 311-312. Translated by Benoy Kumar Sirkar. (Sacred Books of the Hindus.) Cf. Manu. x. 116, where raring of cattle is made one of the principal duties of a Vaisya.

ideas about the province of governmental activity, this piece of legislation was incorporated into state activities. Kautilya deals with a breadth of detail the different methods of the art of cattle-keeping and enjoins upon the Superintendent to see that cows and calves are not put to any inconvenience as regards maintenance and general relief. Towards this effect he recommends a cattle census which would make for greater efficiency as regards the administrative functions of the Superintendent's office. Selling of cows from among the herds is punishable with an amercement of one-fourth of the value of the cow. To improvise sufficient quantity of milk to the calf during the spring and the summer seasons, cows must be milked only one time. In case of default, the cowherd's thumb shall be cut off. " Cattle in calf, a bull, or a milch cow, shall not be slaughtered. He who slaughters or tortures them to death shall be fined 50 panas.'[1] Only fresh and boneless flesh of beasts is to be offered for sale by the butchers under penalty of amercements. In the case of Brahmani bulls set free, the owners must see that they are kept in proper control.[2] Hot spirits among the bulls must not be neglected from being brought under control by " putting a string through the nose of a bull " and are punishable by state intervention.[3] This would mean that havoc capable of being saused by bulls set free is eliminated and thus public property is saved from destruction. This piece of legislation is laudatory in all its

1. *Arthasastra.* Bk. II. Ch. xxvi.
2. *Sukraniti.* I, 622.
3. *Arthasastra.* Bk. II. Ch. xix. Shamasastri p. 158.

detail, and has all the efficiency which a scrutinizing government can bring about.

Along with this, there is the other institution of the Office of the Superintendent of Agriculture, Forest Produce, and Pastures.[1] The functions of these Superintendents are to see that there is a sufficient quantitity of pastures and grasses available for cattle to feed upon. According to Sukra,[2] the place selected for the construction of a city, especially the king's capital, must be "happily provided with resources in grasses and woods." Manu goes even further:[3] "On all sides of a village a space, one hundred dhanus or three sanya-throws (in breadth) shall be reserved (for pasture). and thrice (that space) round a town." The *Dhanus* literally means a bows-length which is four *Hastas* or about six feet in length, and hence the provision for grass lands about every village must be two hundred yards on all sides, which is, taking into consideration the requirements of the livestock in the village, presumably sufficient if not abundant for rural requirements. This is in perfect agreement with what Sukra has to say[4] about the choice of the site for the construction of the metropolis which must be "happily provided with resources in grasses and woods." Kautilya urges that "pasture grounds shall be opened between any two dangerous places" for reasons of a political nature.[5] Such is the importance attached

1. *Ibid.*, Chs, xxiv and xvii and *Sukraniti*, II. 317-19 respectively.
2. *Sukraniti*, I. 425-28.
3. *Laws of Manu.* VIII. 257.
4. *Sukraniti.* I. 425-28.
5. *Arthasastra.* Bk. II. Ch. xxxiv. (Shamasastri p. 172).

to pastures and natural grasses of the conntry in ancient India, that it is quite frequently urged by ancient Indian diplomats and statesmen that one of the effectual weapons to be used in subduing a recalcitrant noble or a dangerous enemy is to reduce their supply of grasses by burning all their pasture lands.[1]

When we trace the history of cow-protection during the period intervening between the death of Asoka and the reign of Harshavardhana, nearly eight and a half centuries, we will be impressed with the fact that it is not favourably comparable with the memorable period of state-action in the cause of cow-protection under the Mauryas. During this period the general movement towards cow-protection has several ebbs. In general we may say that Buddhism remained the moral guide of the populace, with several pit-falls under Pushyamitra Sunga, the Indo-Bactrian kings and even Samudragupta. The supremacy of Buddhism would mean the maintenance of the law of *dharma* which has for its main-spring the glorious principle of *ahimsa.* But under Pushyamitra and even under Samudragupta we find the *aswamedha* sacrifice reviving which is but the indirect expression of Brahmanical influence upon the state.[2] Resort to sacrifice logically leads to the lowering of the ideas about the sanctity of animal life as was inculcated by Jainism and Buddhism. Again, under Mihiragula and the Hun invasions, Buddhism received a rude rocking of its moral endeavours and was practically

1. *Sukraniti.* IV. vii. 740-41.

2. *Early History of India.* By V. A. Smith. 3rd Edn. (1914). pp. 200 and 288, respectively.

crushed under the proud feet of the conquerors[1] even though, later on, it once again revived under the patronage of more liberal kings. Buddhism was unable to maintain its even tenor of life and hence it is natural for us to expect that during this period the general doctrine of *Ahimsa* and *Gorakshan* receded to the background.

But by the time we come to the reign of Harshavardhana, we again find a certain amount of relief and find state-action directing civic action in regard to the sanctity of animal life on earth. Hieun Tsiang informs us that " he prohibited the taking of life under severe penalties and caused the use of animal food to cease throughout the five Indies." [2] The strong incentive to this prohibition of taking animal life is to be found in Harsha's zeal towards Buddhism.

The death of Harshavardhana saw the disintegration of his empire which is the last of the Hindu empires in early Indian history that have reached their zenith successively under Asoka Maurya, Kanishka and Samudragupta. Then set in an era of anarchy and internecine warfare which are but the concomitants of an ever-warring congeries of principalities. During this period, we find the movement towards the protection of animal life beginning its career of waning. Instances of Hindu kings striving towards the preservation and sanctity of animal life are few and far between, while our sources of information are too meagre and fragmentary.

1. *Ibid.* pp. 203 and 319.

2. *Records.* Watters. I. p. 344. Quoted in the *History of Medieval Hindu India.* Vol. I. By Prof: C. V. Vaidya. Cf. Smith. E.H.I. pp. 181 and 344.

Kalhana in his *Rajatarangini* mentions that Gopaditya, a Kasmir king of the sixth century, A.D., "did not tolerate except at sacrifices" "the killing of animals." But the mention of the exception conceded to sacrifices leads us to presume that the legislation of the state is not drastic enough, at least to the desirable extent. But the effort is in itself praiseworthy. Again, in the case of Meghavahana another Kashmiri king, we are informed by Kalhana [2] that "in the reign of this king, who hated killing like a Jaina, the (effigy of an) animal in ghee was used in sacrifice (*Kratu*) and one in pastry at the 'offering to the spirits' (*Bhutabali*)." Jainism is emphatically triumphant here in preaching the most humane doctrine of *ahimsa* and trumpeting the utter futility of sacrifices which are only practical expressions of misdirected outlay and effort. Again, take another passage from the *Rajatarangini* :[3] "On the lake reaching to the brink of the horizon, he established by his own authority a prohibition against the killing of fish and birds, which was to the end of the world." In this case, King Anantivarman of Kasmir (A.D. 855-6 to 883) building a city bearing his name on the banks of Vitasi "where she leaves the waters of the *Mahapadma* (lake)" orders prohibition of killing birds and fish—a supreme act in the cause of *ahimsa*. We need not mention in this connection the sanctity of the cow which will be extremely superfluous.

Our next glimpse we get of the efforts of Kumarapala, King of Gujerat, after his conversion to Jainism in

1. I. 344. Stein. Vol. I. p. 51.
2. *Ibid.* III. 7. *Ibid.* I. 72.
3. V. 119. Stein. Vol. I. p. 201.

A.D 1159. Dr. Smith sums up his efforts in the following passage:[1] "In the twelfth century, Kumarapala, King of Gujerat in Westren India, after his conversion to Jainism in A.D. 1159 took up the doctrine of the sanctity of animal life with the most inordinate zeal, and imposed savage penalties upon the violators of his rules. An unlucky merchant, who had committed the atrocious crime of cracking a louse, was brought before the special court at Anhilwara and punished by the confiscation of his whole property, the proceeds of which were devoted to the building of a temple. Another wretch who had outraged the sanctity of the capital by bringing in a dish of raw meat, was put to death. The special court constituted by Kumarapala had functions similar to those of Asoka's censors, and the working of the latter institution sheds much light upon the unrecorded proceedings of the earlier one." Kumarapala obviously had a strong desire to imitate his predecessor Asoka but in his attempts towards precision he lent himself to overdrawn acts of legislation which are open to objection.

We are now to enter upon that period of Indian history which is replete with instances wherein Muhammadan sovereigns of India who are more liberal than the vast majority of their masses strove their level best towards protecting the cow. Here, I have to make plain the fact that, in view of the evidence furnished in the earlier chapters, however vindictive may have been the nature of the Muhammadan conquering masses and

1. *Early History of India*, p. 181. Smith obtains his information from Buhler's *Ueber Das Leben Des Jaina Monches Hemachandra* (1899).

certain of their fanatic rulers in killing cows, we find brilliant efforts made by some of their illustrious sovereigns of India in the cause of cow protection. These efforts will make us envisage the capabilities of our Muslim neighbours in meeting us at least half way in our efforts to conserve cow life.

To begin with, Babar, the first of the Mughal kings of India, recognised the importance of cow preservation. We cannot exactly vouchsafe for his capabilities to understand the importance of the bovine species to Indian agriculture. But he is quite explicit about the respect towards and sufference of the Hindu reverence towards the cow, of which every Muslim inhabitant of India must be capable. For one thing he never ate beef, but had a partiality towards the flesh of camels. We may read the whole of his *Memoirs* with pleasure but we cannot find a single passage wherein it is mentioned that Babar ate beef. The first Mughal emperor of India is famous for his descriptive detail and imagery. Several feasts and banquets given by him and his subordinate Wazirs were described to the minutest detail but in not even one instance we find beef mentioned as being served to the guests. But, it is far from being a surmise when I say that the Muhammadan stock of Afganstan has a particular partiality towards the flesh of horses and camels. Monserrate mentions[1] that Timur the ancestor of Babar "held frequent banquets at which the flesh of horses was served boiled or roast" in preference to other meats. Babar himself mentions

1. *Commentary of Father Monserrate.* Appendix p. xxx. Translated by J. S. Hoyland. Annotated with introduction by S. N. Banerjee. Humphry Milford. 1922.

quite clearly his relish of camel's flesh. In the valley of Khesh "a fat *Shuterluck* belonging to the Hazaras was found, brought in and killed. We ate part of its flesh roasted, part of it sun-dried (with the rest boiled in vessels). I never ate such fine-flavoured camel's flesh; many could not distinguish it from mutton".[1] This partiality towards camel's flesh is justified by the fact that, as we have already seen in an earlier chapter, the desert Arab was generally habituated to slaughtering camels at sacrifices and banquets.[2]

Babar is more explicit as regards his respect towards the cow. In his death-bed advice to his son Humayun he gives vent to fine sentiments worthy of a genuine follower of Islam. Two copies of the document containing the advice are extant at the present day, the one in the Bhopal State Library and the other in the possession of Principal Balkrishna of the Rajaram College, Kolhapur. The latter one seems to be more complete and I quote it in full.[3] "Secret will of Zahiruddin Mohammed Badashah Ghazi to Prince

1. *Memoirs of Babar.* Vol. I. p. 281. Translated by Leyden and Erskine. Revised by Sir Lucas King, C.S.I., LL. D., F.R.S., Oxford 1921. Shuterluk is a species of camel.

2. *Ante*, chapter on the Muslim Outlook.

3. Dr. Syed Mahmud Ph. D., obtained a photo of the copy preserved in the Bhopal State Library through the courtesy of Nawab Col. Hamid Ullah Khan Sahib and translated it in his article on "Cow-protection under Muslim Rule—a historical survey" in the *Indian Review* for August 1923, which is published as a pamplet for free distribution by the Sri Gorakshak Mandali, Bangalore. The Persian original of Dr. Balkrishna's copy will be shortly published in the Indian Historical Journal. Its translation is practically broadcasted by almost all the news-papers of India in view of the present state of communal riots and polemics over the Bakra-Id Festival.

Nasiruddin Mohammad Humayan, whom God grant a long life, written for the strength of the kingdom :

"O son, the kingdom of India is full of different religions: Praised be God that He bestowed upon thee its sovereignty. It is incumbent on thee to wipe all religious prejudices off the tablet of the heart ; administer justice according to the ways of every religion. Avoid especially the sacrifice of the cow by which thou canst capture the hearts of the peoples of India, and subjects of this country may be bound up with royal obligations.

"Do not ruin the temples and shrines of any community which is obeying the laws of Government. Administer justice in such a manner that the king be pleased with the subjects and the subjects with the king. The cause of Islam can be promoted by the sword of obligations than by the sword of tyranny.

"Overlook the dissensions of the Shias and Sunnis, else the weakness of Islam is manifest.

"And let the subjects of different beliefs be harmonised in conformity with the four elements (of which) the human body is harmoniously composed, so that the body of the kingdom may be free from different diseases. The Memoirs of Timur, the master of conjunction (i.e., fortune) should always be before thine eye, so that thou mayest become experienced in the affairs of administration." Ist. Jamadi-ul Awwal, 935 A.H.

The reigns of Humayun and Sher Shah may well be skipped over as they are not quite so important to our present purpose, and are mainly occupied with defeats, flights, conquests and reconquests, which would mean loss of equilibrium in the State. When we come to Akbar we have perhaps as persistent a sovereign in the cause of cow-protection as Asoka.

Akbar's ecclecticism and strong leanings towards Hinduism are quite plain even to the superfluous reader of history. His broadmindedness, his catholic policy, his openness to new impressions, were instrumental in bringing about his policy of religious tolerance. Theologians and *muftis*, logicians and scholars of varying attainments and belonging to different religions and creeds assembled round him in the spacious *Ibadat Khana* or House of Worship at Fatepur Sikri built in 1575. The *pros* and *cons* of dogmas were carefully hearkened to by this excessively inquisitive monarch, however intricate their logical catechism, however subtle their metaphysical abstraction. His openness of mind was such that different religions claimed in him a proselyte. Monserrate the Jesuit Missionery claims that he embraced the path of Jesus of Nazareth, while the Jains equally justify their claims in maintaining the conversion of Jalal-uddin Akbar, to the creed of Mahavira. However this may be, which is a matter to be decided by scholars, this much is certain that Akbar had strong leanings towards Zoroastrianism, and more particularly towards Jainism.

Akbar is positive as regards his distaste of flesh. Whether this is due to the Jain influence on him or to instinctive moral repugnance and sensitiveness to see a brute butchered, we cannot ascertain. But this much is plain that his instinct of humanitarianism is as strong as that of any Jain. Take this passage from the *Ain-I-Akbari* :[1] "His Majesty has a great disinclination for flesh: and he frequently says, 'Providence has prepared variety of food for man, but, through ignorance and gluttony, he destroys living creatures, and makes his body a tomb for beasts. If I were not a king, I would leave off eating flesh at once, and now it is my intention to quit it by degrees.' For sometime, he abstained from flesh on Fridays ; then on Sundays: now, on the first day of every solar month, and on Sundays, and on the days of the eclipses of the sun and of the moon, and the day between two Sufyanehs ;[2] and the Mondays of the month Rajeb, and the festival of the month Teer, together with the whole of the month Fervirdeen (March), and the month in which His Majesty was born, which is Aban (October). And it being ordered, that the Sufyanhe should last for as many days as his Majesty was years old, some days in the next month Azer were likewise added ; and now the whole of this last month is Sufyaneh and out of his righteousness, besides all these, it is still increasing some days every year, and never less than five days."

This is but a significant passage testifying to his strong beliefs about the sanctity of animal life. But, for his legislation in the cause of cow-protection we have to go in else-where.

1. Page 56. Translated by Francis Gladwin. I hope to supply references from Blochmann and Jarret, in a future edition of this work, as they are not available to me at present in this part of the mufassil.

2. That is, if a day intervened between two days that were appointed for abstaining from flesh, that intermediate day became also Sufyaneh.

Here I am to note that Akbar remitted several vexatious taxes including taxes on the sale and slaughter of cattle and the one for dressing hides.[1] This would mean the relaxation of state control over important transactions which are sure to touch the economics of the state. From very early times of Muhammadan rule in India, we find these taxes are collected vigorously to conserve cattle life. Dr. Syed Mahmud sums up this piece of legislation in the following manner :[2] "From the very inception of Muslim rule a special tax was imposed on butchers for the slaughter of cows to the extent of 12 "Jetal" per cow. During the reign of Feroz Shah, butchers complained against this tax and the king abolished it. Details of this taxation are not given in books of history, but its object could only have been the prevention of cow slaughter. This tax, therefore, continued for two hundred years after the establishment of Muslim rule in India, right up to the time of Feroz Shah Tughlak. Instead of issuing a general order prohibiting cow slaughter, this was the method adopted by early Mohammedan kings. This tax was called Jazri. At the time of Mohammad Shah Tughlak, beef was not cooked in the royal kitchen, and the king did not take it. Several authors have given detailed description of the royal kitchen, but there is no mention of slaughtering cows. Farhat-ul-Mulk was appointed Governor of Gujerat, and continued in that capacity also during the reign of the next king Mohamed Ghias-ud-Din Tughlak, the Second. Historians state that Farhat-ul-Mulk made

---

1. *Ibid* p. 248.

2. Cow Protection under Muslim Rule—A Historical Survey. *Indian Review* for August 1923.

various concessions to the Hindus, and did not allow the slaughter of cows. The Hindus wielded great influence during the reign of Sultan Nasir-ud-Din Khushro. This king totally stopped the killing of cows in his territories. It also seems that the Jazari tax which had been discontinued by Feroz Shah Tughlak, was re-imposed after his reign, because it is recorded in books of history that Akbar abrogated this tax. Akbar ordered a total prohibition of the killing of cows, and the tax was no longer found necessary and it was probably on that account that it was discontinued."

When we place the above injunctions of Akbar alongside of the attempts of his predecessors, we may not be impressed with this legislation of his who is famous for his partiality towards the cow. As a matter of fact, Akbar has no necessity to protect the cow by means of this paltry and indirect method of legislation. On the other hand, his cow-protection policy is broad-based and comprehensive. He is overt in his favour of the Hindu, the Jain and the Zoroastrian creeds. History proves his several concessions to these creeds which were granted in good faith. His partiality towards Jainism is quite marked, and his declarations about using meat as an article of food, quoted above, are quite in assonance with this particular bent of his mind.

We have corroborative evidence that three Jain gurus attended the court of Akbar and ministered unto his mental inquisitiveness in hankering after information about the different religions of the world. Hiravijaya Suri, Vijayasena Suri and Bhanuchandra Upadhyaya are credited to have exercised a wholesome influence upon Akbar, and obtained a *firman* prohibiting under penalty of capital punishment animal slaughter in general and cow slaughter in particular.[1] This *firman* is preserved on the walls of a porch to the Adiswara Temple on the Satrunjaya Hills close to Palitana State in the Kathiawad. Dr. Buhler sums up this long inscription in the following manner:[2] "*Hiravijaya* (Klatt No. 58), verses 14-24, who was called by Sahi Akabbara (Shah Akbar to Mevata, and persuaded the emperor in Samvat 1639) A.D. 1582 to issue an edict forbidding the slaughter of animals for six months, to abolish the confiscation of the property of deceased persons, the *Sujijia* tax, and a *Sulka*; to set free many captives, snared birds and animals; to present Satrunjaya to the Jainas; to establish a Jaina library (*Pustaka Bhandagaram*), and to become a saint like king Srenika; who converted the head of the Lumpakas, Meghaji; made many people adherents of the Tapagachchha; caused many temples to be built in Gujarat and other countries; and many natives of that country, of Malva, and so forth, undertake pilgrimages to Satrunjaya. No. CXVIII commemorates one of these pilgrimages, which was undertaken by Hiravijaya belonged to the *Sapha* race. He died, according to XIII by starvation at Unnatadurga, in Samvat 1652, Bhadra-

1. *Bhandarkar Commemoration Volume* pp. 265-276. Article on the Jain Teachers of Akbar by V. A. Smith. Bhandarkar Oriental Institute, of Poona. 1917.

2. *Ibid* pp. 272-273. Being not in possession of either Keilhorne's or Buhler's collection of inscriptions I was not able to give the full text of the inscription here. I hope to do so in a second edition of the monograph. Cf. The same is summed up by S. N. Bannerjee in his introduction to the *Commentary of Father Monserrate.* pp. iv and v.

pada Sukla 10, and his *Padukas* were erected in the same year, on Marga-vadi 9, Monday, by Udayakarana of Stambhatirtha (Cambay) and consecreated by Vijayasena. (4) (Klatt No. 59), (verses 25-34), who was called by Akabbara (Akbar) to Labhapura (Lahor), received from him great honours, and a *Phuramana* (*Farman*), forbidding the slaughter of cows, bulls, and buffalo-cows, to confiscate the property of deceased persons and to make captives in war; who, honoured by the king, the son of Choli-begam (Choli Vegama), adorned Gujarat. Latest date Samvat 1650."

A similar account has been furnished by a modern writer on mountain temples and historical inscriptions on their porches. Summarising the series of inscriptions on the temples of the Shatrunjaya hills which comprise the *Firmans* of Mughal sovereigns of India in their efforts to bring about mutual amity and concord between Hindus and Muhammadans, Mr. G. K. N. writes in the *Bombay Chronicle*: [1] "There is first of all the *Firman* of Jellaludin Muhammad Akbar. It guarantees the Jains the maintenance of their worship and the exercise of their religion and doctrine 'throughout our Empire and dominions.' Something more important follows,—that no one can kill an animal on those mountains or temples or below or about them. It is but proper that the Jain should perform his devotions with composure of heart. 'Let no one ever oppose or make objection' to the decree. Let the orders contained in the *Firman* be acted upon and carried out.

"The second edict is from the Emperor Jahangir in similar terms.

1 Quoted in *The Muslim Outlook*. p. 7. April 8, 1926, Lahore

"The third *Firman* is from Shahjehan who confirms the preceding documents. Then we have another of the same Emperor granting greater liberty. He emphasises that every year a new order shall not be demanded but that those whom it concerns shall not swerve from what is here commanded. A further 'world-binding mandate' is issued by another Padishah, one more the 'Dar-ul-Khilafat', proving that at times the Indian Emperors considered themselves rightful Khalifas. The documents are too interesting to be dismissed with a curt notice. .... It must have been an India in those days certainly immune from that fierce acerbity between the Hindus and Musalmans which seems now to usurp their minds to the exclusion of true national endeavours".

From this evidence it is positively clear that Akbar had very strong ideas about cow-protection from several view-points. Firstly he is instinctively repugnant to partake of flesh from the humanitarian point of view, as his declarations about meat-eating and his abstinence from eating flesh would clearly prove. Next to this, his respect for the feelings of his Hindu subjects and his leanings towards the *Ahimsa* principle of Jainism influenced him to order prohibition of cow-slaughter in his dominions. Possibly he might have had strong notions about the economic relationship of the cow-protection problem to the country's needs.

Akbar's policy is maintained and perpetuated by his successors. Jehangir who is a mixture of extremes, and Aurangzib who is notoriously known to have done the greatest harm to the progress of Hinduism are famous for their efforts to save the cow's life. The Shatrunjaya

Inscription mentions Jehangir's *Firman* to protect cow-life which is in complete harmony with that of his father Abkar. [1] Further, he is credited with having stopped all slaughter of animals and all manner of hunting on Sundays to commemorate Akbar's birth-day, and on Thursdays as a token of Almighty's grace in consecrating him King, on that day.[2] On this point, Bernier, the French Traveller who visited the Mughal court during the years 1656-1668 is more explicit. After referring to the sacredness of the cow in the eyes of the Hindus, Bernier continues :[3] " It ought likewise to be observed that owing to the great deficiency of pasture land in the *Indies* it is impossible to maintain large numbers of cattle ; the whole therefore would soon disappear if animal food were eaten in anything like the proportion in which it is consumed in *France* and *England*, and the country would thus remain uncultivated. The heat is so intense, and the ground so parched, during eight months of the year, that the beasts of the field, ready to die of hunger, feed on every kind of filth like so many swine. It was on account of the scarcity of cattle that *Jehan-Guyre*, at the request of the *Brahmens*, issued an edict to forbid the killing of beasts of pasture for a certain number of years :"

The reign of Aurangzib is noted for the internecine quarrels among the different principalities dispersed over the length and breadth of the country and the

---

1 *Ibid.*

2 Dr. Syed Mahmud in the *Indian Review* For August 1923, on 'Cow-protection under Muslim rule—a historical survey.'

3 *Travels in the Mogul Empire.* p. 236. Translated by Archibald Constable. Revised by V. A. Smith, 1914. Oxford. Humphrey Milford.

attempts of the Mughal *Padshahi* to subdue them on the one hand, and the civil war that ultimately gave him the reigns of government after a huge flow of blood. The concomitant of war would be loss of life, human and animal. Especially in medieval warfare the beast played a prominent part. Besides the elephant and the horse the Bull played a unique part as a beast of burden. These wars of Aurangzib caused serious loss of animal life, and this has been graphically described by Manucci in his *Storia to mogar* :[1] " Instead of verdure all is blank and barren. The country is so entirely desolated and depopulated that neither fire nor light can be found in the course of a three or four days' journey. . . . There have died in his armies a hundred thousand souls yearly, and of animals, pack oxen, camels, elephants etc., over three hundred thousand." Commenting upon this phenomena Bernier points out, [2] after his reference to Jehangir's prohibition of the slaughter of beasts of pasture, that " not long since they presented a similar petition to *Aureng-Zebe*, offering him a considerable sum of money to ensure his compliance. They argued that the neglected and the ruinous condition of many tracts of country during the last fifty or sixty years was attributable to the paucity and dearness of oxen." According to *islami Gorakshan*, later Mughal sovereigns of India such as Muhammad Shah and Shah Alam prohibited cow slaughter.[3]

1. *Storia do Mogor*. iv. 252 and 96. Quoted in the *History of Aurangzib*. Vol. V. p. 236. By Jadunath Sarkar, M. A., Calcutta, 1924.

2. *Travels in the Mogal Empire*. pp. 326-327.

3. p. 41.

Muhammadan sovereigns of India were famous for their policy of give and take and the appreciation of the Hindu beliefs in the sanctity of the cow. Further, they were fully cognisant of the fact that the solidarity of the state depended upon the peace and good-will between the Hindus and the Muslims. They conceded the fact that cow-slaughter was never a tenet of Islam. To crown all, they prohibited any recrimination on the part of the conqueror Muslims and preached the wholesome gospel of the value of animal life, in particular of cow-life. If the masses of the Muslim population of India at the present day are made to realise and appreciate this legacy of history which their co-religionists that have gone by have lent to posterity, then the cow-protection problem in India would have been completely solved.

Our next glimpse in the cause of cow-protection we get from the inspirational declarations and achievements of Sivaji, who is hailed by the Hindu population of India as an incarnation of God—Sabhasad maintains in his *Siva Chhatrapati* that Shree Sambhu Mahadev declared himself incarnate in the person of Sivaji,[1] to deliver the Brahman and the cow from the clutches of the Muhammadan population of India. Sivaji personally justifies this belief. When he was taken against his will to the *Durbar* of the Sultan of Bijapur at the age of twelve to obtain his favours, Sivaji declares : "[2] "We are Hindus and they Yavanas. They are very

1. *Siva Chhatrapati* by Krishnaji Anant Sabhasad, Translated from the Maratha Bakhar, by Surendranath Sen. Calcutta University. 1920. p. 2.

2, *Chitnis Bakhar*. p. 27. Translated in *Ibid*. p. 160.

low in fact there is none lower,—I feel a loathing to salute them. They commit evil deeds like cow-slaughter. It is wrong to witness any slight on religion and the Brahmans. Cows are slaughtered as we pass by the roads. It pains me and I feel inclined to cut off the head of the offender. In my mind I feel disposed to decapitate the oppressor of the cows but I am helpless as I do not know what my father will think of it." Again, when the Padshah talks of remarrying Sivaji as his first marriage was, as he vouches, a mere play, Sivaji argues according to the *Siva Digvijaya*;[1] "We are Hindus and the rightful lords of the realm, it is not proper for us to witness cow slaughter and oppression of the Brahmans." Sivaji's later policy and achievements justify this personal dogma of his. But his enthusiasm and sacred duty to protect the Cow and the Brahman never led him to indiscriminate slaughter of the Muhammadans even during the height of his military achievements.

At the disintegration of the Mughal, the Vijayanagar and the Maratha empires, we have to stop for a time in our sketch of the history of cow-protection in India. Our sources of information fail us here. The country is immersed throughout the eighteenth and the earlier half of the nineteenth centuries in a series of wars. One by one the empires crumble. The British had begun to exchange their trade for the sword. Gradually they became masters of India. During this period, no single ruler, Hindu or otherwise, was able to bestow particular attention towards the cow,—at least, our source books fail us here in this respect, as he was completely absorbed

1. p. 111. quoted in *Ibid*, p. 160.

in his attempts to prevent the sword of the conqueror from exterminating his dynasty and escheat his estate. But all the same, the feelings of the Hindus were ever strong in favour of respecting cow-life. The mere suspicion, alleged or actual, that the fat of the cow was used in preparing the cartridges for the Enfield Rifle drove into fury the Hindu Sepoys in the British service, and set into a blaze all the fires of the sentimental clingings of the Hindus at the time of the Sepoy Mutiny. This is evidence positive of the staunch beliefs of the Hindus in imputing sanctity to the cow, which always goaded them to constrain the state to see that their wholesome beliefs in this respect are never abrogated, while nothing prejudicial to the cause of cow-protection ever happens through the instrumentality of the state.

In quite recent years Kasmir and Nepal stand prominent in their efforts towards cow-protection. The strange factor to be borne in mind is that Kasmir is predominently Muhammadan, while Nepal is a comparatively undeveloped state when compared with India proper and is situated in an extremely mountainous zone. Kasmir seems to have been perpetuating her policy towards protecting the cow as propounded by her Meghavahanas and Anantivarmans of yore, as we have seen above. The *Ranvir Danda Vidhi* provides:[1]

"Section 219.—Slaughter or Murder of a Cow or like animal. If any person intentionally kills or slaughters any animal of kine division, either the cow or bull,

1. Quoted in the Memorial to H. H. the Maharaja of Mysore by the Sree Gorakshak Mandali, Bangalore praying for cow protection.

he will be subjected to punishment. Either of the two kinds of imprisonments the terms of which may be up to 10 years, can be inflicted and a fine will also be imposed according to circumstances.

"Explanation :—The word cow includes *Gonda* or wild cow also.

"If any person keeps the flesh of any animal referred to in Section 219, in his possession knowing it or having reasons to believe that it is of any such animal, he will be punished. Either of the two kinds of imprisonments the terms of which may be up to one year and a fine up to Rs. 500 will also be imposed according to circumstances.

"Section 219B.—If any person slaughters or kills any she-buffalo, a fine will be imposed. The amount of the fine can be upto five times the value of the animal (which the Court may fix).

"Procedure :—The offence under this Section is interferable by Police, unbailable, and uncompoundable, and will be tried by a First Class Magistrate."

Likewise is the case of Nepal. Nurtured in the lap of fervent Buddhism for ages and having imbibed to the core the Aryan partiality towards the cow, the Nepalese are to-day staunch cow-protectors. As Sir Bampfylde Fuller puts it, "Cow killing is under its strictest interdict among the Mongolian people of Nepal." [1]

In the State of Jodhpur there is a long standing order prohibiting the slaughter of cows. In the light of

1. *Studies in Indian Life and Sentiments* p. 103, Murray (1910).

the latest information, even the export of cows, female sheep and she-goats is prohibited.[1] Again, the Maharaja of Sondur State in the Bellary District declared recently at Devangre that the slaughter of cows shall be forbidden in his state, and that old and dry animals in the hands of itinerant butchers, if they happen to pass through his territory would be liberated at the cost of the state.[2] Both these instances are commendable. Even Provincial Governments of British India are seen to be sympathetic towards the prevention of cow-slaughter. For example, Order No. 1236-955—XIII of the Central Provinces Government dated 31-5-1922, prohibitted the killing of cows in the licensed as well as private slaughter houses situated within their jurisdiction. It is hoped that other provincial Governments would soon follow suit and penalise cow-slaughter.

The cow-protection movement in India at the present day is purely one of education and propaganda. Several undesirable elements have cropped up to stop the general progress of cow-protection, such as the Muslim obstinacy in maintaining the indispensability of cows for sacrificial purposes and the economic arguments of the burden upon the farmer of sterile and aged cows if they are to be fed in their useless old age. The movement at the present day has swelled in volume, while its outlook and range of activities have broadened. Propaganda has been carried on on an extensive scale. Sterling facts about cow-protection which are capable of lifting up the screen of prejudice and ignorance have been broad-cast. Literature bearing upon the different problems connected

1. Memorial of the Gorakshak Mandali.
2. *Social Reformer*. p. 392. February 30, 1926.

with cow-protection in India has been made accessible to the public though on a modest scale. Communal feelings and petty prejudices and provincialism of creed-dogmas have been at present drawing the attention of the cultured who are trying to obliterate them.

Towards this effect, propaganda has been extensively carried on. The cow-conference has been organised along with the annual sessions of the Indian National Congress. There is a Central Cow-Protection Society for India organised under the kind patronage of Mr. M. K. Gandhi known as All India Cow-protection Society with its head-quarters at Sabarmati. Besides this there are several societies in India[1] conducting their operations mainly depending upon their own resources and equipment. The following societies deserve mention :

The Society for the Prevention of Cruelty to Animals stands out as the oldest humanitarian institution in India. It was started at Madras in the year 1877, by Mr. William Digby C. I. E., with His Grace the Duke of Buckingham and Chandos as first patron and Lady Grenville as first patroness. All these fifty years the Society has been pushing on its propaganda with unremitting zeal. But the operations of the Society do not limit themselves to the cause of cow-protection alone. On the other hand, the outlook of the Society is very broad and includes all branches of humanitarian work. The Society's inspectors have the powers of the police authorities in booking all classes of people without

---

1. All these societies were good enough to appreciate my appeal for information and guidance. I must sincerely acknowledge their sympathy and assistance, but for which my enthusiasm would nearly have been chilled.

distinction of status, if ever they are caught red-handed in acts of cruelty to animals. It has seven branches in the Madras Presidency and has the backing of highly influential men in the Presidency.

Next in priority of birth comes the Islami Gorakshan Office at Sitapore, U. P. The Society is the out-come of the efforts of Mr.Syed Nazir Ahmed Saheb, a prominent Vakil of Sitapore. Born in 1872 and belonging to the Shia set of the Muslims. Mr. Nazir Ahmed was fully imbued with respect towards the cow and deep feelings of respect towards Gopalak Sri Krishnaji heartily and sincerely", to quote his nephew's letter to the present writer. His mission is simply to demonstrate that cow-slaughter is in no way a tenet of Islamic creed. Towards this, he entered upon a career of propaganda preaching to the masses the value of cow-protection. He strove his level best to disseminate correct information about the theological position of the cow in different religions, especially from the Muslim view-point. He published several pamphlets about this subject and permanently established the Islami Gorakshan Office at Sitapur to carry on propaganda work in the cause of cow-protection.

The Cow-Preservation League, Calcutta was started in 1922 under the distinguished presidency of the late Sir Asutosh Mukherjee to propagate the cause of cow-protection. It is at present managed by a strong directorate of enthusiasts under the presidency of the Hon'ble Justice Sir Nalini Ranjan Chaterjee. It has got a network of branches throughout the whole of India, in all sixty societies. This League is noted for its assiduity in collecting information and statistics from the different parts of India. This organisation shows clearly what a centralised and co-ordinated institution can accomplish in the cause of doing good to the country.

Shree Ghatkopar Sarvajanika Jivadaya Khata, or the Ghatkopar Humanitarian Association of Bombay is doing prominent work in this line in western India. With a panel of influential Marwari merchants for its promoters, and with an ardent enthusiast in Mr. Manecklal A. Mehta as Secretary, the Association is doing excellent work ever since its inception in 1923. The main object of the Society is the saving of milch cattle from going to the Bombay slaughter-houses, besides propaganda work.

Sree Gorakshak Mandali of Bangalore city is a prominent institution in the South. With Diwan Bahadur Rajasabhabhushana Sir K. P. Puttanna Chetti, C.I.E., and Shah Chimanmal Dongaji for its President and Secretary respectively, the association has been doing appreciable work in Mysore and the South. The Mandali memorialised the liberal Maharaja about issuing a prohibitory order to stop cow-slaughter in his dominions. Much is expected from this.

Besides this, there have been started in India several other propagandist societies of minor importance in name but never in genuine exertion. The prosperity of India lies in societies such as these and the patriots who are at their helm.

The history of the *Pinjrapole* and its place in Indian life is noteworthy. That this is an extremely old institution, no one can deny. Tradition and present-day manifestations confirm this. But in view of the paucity of material at our disposal, anything like a comprehensive survey of the history of this charitable institution is a difficult task. In the chapter on the Buddhist attitude we have briefly adverted to the institutions of the *Pinjrapole* and maintained the thesis that Buddhism had had her indelible impression upon the conduct and type of the *Pinjrapole*. Dr. D. R. Bhandarkar sums up this feature of the institution in the following brilliant passage:[1] " As regards the *Pinjrapoles* or animal hospitals, they are found to this day in Western India. The earliest description of a *Pinjrapole* is that furnished by Hamilton and is of one that was maintained at Surat late in the eighteenth century. Any animal with a broken limb or otherwise disabled is admitted without any regard to the caste or nationality of its master. This suits here excellently. For, when Asoka says that he organised medical treatment for both man and animal, what he means is that in the case of the former he established charitable dispensaries for distributing medicine gratis and in the case of the latter something like a *Pinjrapole*. When again he says that medicinal herbs, roots and fruits were imported and planted where they did not exist previously, we are to understand that he estabished farms attached to those institutions so that all medicines might be there for ready use. It is indeed curious to find that the custom of giving free medical relief to the diseased man or animal which was in existence in West India in the eighteenth century was prevalent as early as the third

1. *Carmichael Lectures on Asoka.* pp, 185-186. Calcutta (1925).

century B. C. And what is still further noteworthy is that through the philanthropic activity of Asoka all the drugs then known were made available to the world."

This is from the institutional point of view. On the other side of medical treatment and its history, the Thakore Saheb of Gondol maintains[1] that "Veterinary Science seems to have been highly cultivated long before that period (Mahabharata). Nala, a remote ancestor of the Pandavas is described as a most accomplished horse-trainer, and as possessing a thorough knowledge of all matters relating to the horse. Nakula, one of the five Pandavas, was expert in the veterinary science, on which he has written several works, his "Aswa-chikitsa" being still extant. The science of treating elephants, bullocks and other domestic animals, was and is still known in India. Some are of opinion that Vagbhata the celebrated author of "Ashtangahradya," flourished at the time of Mahabharata, and that he was the family physician of the Pandavas.

"In the time of Buddha (B.C. 543), Indian medicine received the greatest support and stimulus, and surgery was allowed to languish. For Buddha and his followers would not permit the dissection of animals. They put a stop to animal sacrifice, in which a knowledge of anatomy was indispensable, and substituted models of dough. Buddha, however, established hospitals for men and beasts all over the country, and the institution of Pinjrapoles (Animal hospitals), so peculiar to India, owes its origin to him."

1. *A short history of Aryan medical science.* pp. 188-189.

The institution of the *Pinjrapole* is perpetuated in India to the present-day. It is but a common sight in Bombay to see a few cows gathered before a Marwari or Gujarati gentleman's house where are provided ample supplies of grass to these sacred beasts. Pure milk is only to be got at these *Pinjrapoles* [1] conducted on a very modest scale and dispersed all over the city. This personal observation of the present writer seems to justify the above contentions of Dr. D. R. Bhandarkar. But the *Pinjrapoles* do not seem to have been fully developed throughout the country on really efficacious lines, while they seem to be not exactly popular as their number is quite modest. The development of this institution is fraught with very good results and it is a desirable institution to be fully developed.

I will now close this chapter with a brief description of the animal hospital of the Jains at Allahabad which shows the amity existing between man and beast in India. Mr. L. Moresby writes in the *Herald of the Golden Age* : [2] " In Ahmadabad I visited the Jain Hospital for animals—a most wonderful and touching place. It is a compound in the midst of the city with trees in it and large sheds where the sick and wounded animals are tended. The pariah dogs in India are a very painful sight—so lean and starved that their ribs stand out like the ribs of a stranded hulk ; so ravenous that they run beside the train as it leaves a station, watching with famished eyes for morsels that some kind hand but

1. *Pinjrapole* is used here as is passed off generally, as a place where cows are gathered either for milking or feeding.

2. Vol. XVI. Quoted in *The Jaina Gazette*. Vol. XXI. No. 7. July, 1925. pp. 208-209.

seldom throws. Here I saw some lying contentedly with their puppies nestling beside them, and food before them fresh from the great cauldrons in which it is boiled for all the guests are tended and cared for as part of our common brother-hood. Beside them was standing a bullock, with shining coat like grey velvet and a cruel scar healing along his flank. Above in the trees the grey monkeys chattered and held out tiny black paws for alms. The goats stood by with their kids, and men and boys went about feeding and tending them, and I have seldom seen a happier place (though indeed there were sights of suffering), because it seemed to re-knit the bond between man and beast and to speak of a debt owed for faithful service, and therefore ungrudgingly paid."

ERRATA

In page	Line	For	Read
9	17	has	had
18	7	unnecessary	unnecessarily
23	21	materialisatic	materialistic
24	24	Starvation.	Starvation,
25	21	inense	intense
28	7	salutory	salutary
31	5	doctrinnaire	doctrinaire
31	26	decadance	decadence
44	5	prevelance	prevalence
46	17	sacrificies	sacrifices
55	8	creater	creator
64	13	it	its
69	5	completly	completely
70	22	proferred	profferred
75	22	Arayan	Aryan
77	28	Zaroastrian	Zoroastrian
81	10	deavour	devour
83	3	sacrificiol	sacrificial
85	2	*heards*	*herds*
85	16	purficatory	purificatory
91	4	decadant	decadent
92	20	,,	,,
94	25	aencdotes	anecdotes
95	15	He	His
,,	16	collosal	colossal
,,	19	durings	during
,,	25	permanant	permanent
96	32	fine	time
,,	,,	move	more
100	5	dif!erence	differenee
,,	13	schemin	scheming
,,	18	Hindustans	Hindustan
101	29	ubiquous	ubiquitous
103	15	ot	of
104	17	sereen	screen
105	23	unecessarily	unnecessarily
111	11	Prophat	Prophet
,,	,,	Advice	Advise
,,	12	to patriots	patriots to
,,	30	duringd	during
113	13	infidelitey	infidelity
119	13	hatered	hatred
,,	15	,,	,,

ERRATA

In Page	Line	For	Read
120	3	commnnity	community
121	2	pratice	practice
,,	17	beneficient	beneficent
,,	20	make	makes
,,	21	scence the	scent of the
,,	29	admirable	admirably
122	2	life	the life
,,	24	Production	Protection
,,	26	as	is
123	5	oddites	oddities
,,	12	cow-slaugter	cow-slaughter
126	29	originaly	originally
132	11	levened	leavened
133	3	in side	inside
,,	16	front our	front of our
134	4	grievences	gricvances
,,	20	of	or
137	17	man	men
143	15	gumbled	grumbled
144	17	presence two	presence of two
145	20	tho pole aze	the pole axe
148	9	obstinence	abstinence
149	5	maintance	maintenance
	16	diognosis	diagnosis
	21	poutice	poultice
151	21	strong thening	strengthening
153	7	metullurgy	metallurgy
	28	*Beast and Man India*	*Beast and Man in India*
155	32	archieves	archives
156	21	certains	contains
159	6	dysentary	dysentery
160	1	trancendent	transcendent
161	28	deliquents	delinquents
164	25	word	world
,,	32	decadant	decadent
165	22	Venetion	Venetian
166	17	observe	observes
,,	24	phenomna	phenomena
168	15	memarable	memorable
,,	21	npon	upon
169	12	ivasion	invasion
170	1	socialogical	sociological
,,	9	endevour	endeavour
171	15	aud	and
173	26	saused	caused
175	1	conntry	country
182	6	ecclecticism	eclecticism